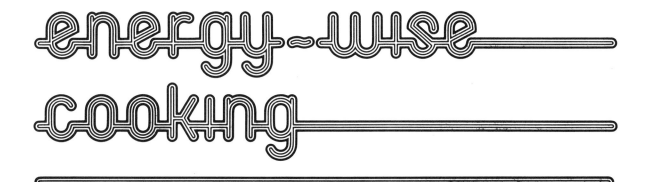

energy-wise cooking

CUT ENERGY COSTS WITH THESE SENSATIONAL RECIPES

margaret happel

Butterick Publishing

The author and publisher thank the following for supplying props for use in the photography: La Cuisinière, 867 Madison Ave., New York, NY 10021; Manhattan Ad Hoc Housewares, 842 Lexington Ave., New York, NY 10021; The Pottery Barn, 321 Tenth Ave., New York, NY 10011; and Villeroy and Boch, 41 Madison Ave., New York, NY 10010.

Book Design: *Betty Binns*

Photography: *Bill Helms*

Pictured on the front cover: Veal Birds (page 26), Glazed Acorn Squash (page 25) and Irish Soda Bread (page 25).

Library of Congress Cataloging in Publication Data

Happel, Margaret.
  Energy-wise cooking.

  Includes index.
  1. Cookery.   2. Energy conservation.   I. Title.
TX652.H365   641.5   79-51220
ISBN 0-88421-065-0

CONTENTS

introduction

As we're all aware, the era of cheap, plentiful energy has gone the way of the dinosaur. Does this mean a return to open-hearth cooking? Not at all. By rethinking our cooking methods, we can conserve precious fuels and still enjoy 20th-century conveniences. In fact, saving energy can be easier than following our customary energy-squandering kitchen practices.

ENERGY-WISE COOKING reveals how to use your kitchen appliances for peak efficiency—with delicious results. For example, just one of the energy-wise oven practices you'll find here is "oven management" of complete menus. All the dishes are popped into the oven—and ready at the same time. When you don't need the whole oven, turn to the toaster oven chapter with its recipes for everything from hors d'oeuvres to an entire meal for two.

Main dishes, side dishes and complete meals can be prepared with little energy on the top of your stove or in the electric skillet, as the chapters on these appliances show. And ENERGY-WISE COOKING brings back the pressure cooker, which can produce such delights as Creole Pork Chops and Apple Brown Betty with a fraction of the time and energy otherwise required.

You'll also find recipes for the champion energy saver, the slow cooker, which can serve up a variety of tasty, hearty dishes. And this book would not be complete without recipes for that energy-saving wonder of the modern kitchen, the microwave oven.

So read on. While you're cutting your energy bills, you'll discover new and easy kitchen practices. Even better, you'll discover the wide range of delicious, family-style food that energy-efficient cooking can make.

The next time you're jockeying the holiday turkey to make space for the baked potatoes, the candied yams and the last-minute apple pie, remember that this is probably one of the few times you're using your oven at its maximum efficiency. Whether it's a Sunday roast or a lone meat pie, most of us just turn the oven dial without a thought as to how to use all that hot, empty space economically.

We all enjoy a break from the daily routine of cooking meals, especially during the hot summer months. Get around this chore by "cooking once, serving twice"—making hot and cold variations of certain favorite dishes. As any meat loaf aficionado knows, a great debate rages over the merits of a hot, juicy loaf versus the chilled, savory variety. But did you realize that Wine-Flavored Flank Steak and Savory Meat Pies, just to name two, are also delicious hot or cold? Even if you can't abide leftovers, you'll find nothing stale or ho-hum about these zesty suggestions for serving chilled entrées with snappy salads and crunchy breads.

You don't feel it's a meal unless it's hot? Double-batching has been around for years as a boon for those busy days when you're pressed for time to cook. Did you know it's a great energy saver too? Included in the following pages are all kinds of tempting recipes that will serve four people twice.

As we all know from our holiday experiences, the oven is capable of much more than just heating a single course. In fact, it can easily handle a complete menu. So you'll find some suggestions for "oven management"—preparing a complete meal by using just one source of heat. Once you get the hang of it, you'll be able to come up with your own energy-efficient menu schemes.

Whether you have a fondness for hot and crispy fried chicken or cool, creamy chicken salad; or you hanker after a hot meal tonight and a quick supper on "one of those days"—turn the page and enjoy!

roast beef and creamy mustard sauce

5-pound rolled rump roast
2 teaspoons salt
½ teaspoon pepper

SAUCE

1½ cups sour cream
¼ cup prepared spicy mustard
2 tablespoons horseradish, drained

1. Wipe beef well with damp paper towels; sprinkle all surfaces of roast with salt and pepper. Place on wire rack on roasting pan; insert meat thermometer into thickest part of roast.

2. Roast at 325° F for 2½ to 3 hours or until meat thermometer reads 150° to 170° F. Let stand for 10 minutes at room temperature before carving.

3. Meanwhile, make sauce by combining sour cream, mustard and drained horseradish in medium bowl. Divide between two serving bowls and chill. Serve half of beef as an entrée with one bowl of sauce alongside.

To serve cold: Cool and chill remaining beef. Serve as cold entrée with chilled sauce and tomato salad. Or serve as sandwich filling using sauce as a topping.

Each half serves 4.

wine-flavored flank steak

2-pound flank steak
½ cup olive or vegetable oil
¼ cup dry red wine or red wine vinegar
1 clove garlic, crushed
½ teaspoon salt
¼ teaspoon pepper

1. Wipe steak well with damp paper towels. Using very sharp knife, lightly score both sides of steak into pattern of 1-inch diamonds.

2. In large shallow glass baking dish, combine oil, red wine or vinegar, garlic, salt and pepper. Add steak to marinade; turn to coat well. Cover and chill for 2 hours, turning meat frequently.

3. Preheat broiler.

4. Remove steak from marinade; reserve marinade. Broil steak 3 inches from heat, 3 to 5 minutes per side. Brush frequently with marinade.

5. Cut steak across grain into thin slices. Serve half immediately.

To serve cold: Arrange remaining flank steak slices on platter; pour a little reserved marinade over steak. Chill. Serve as salad, accompanied by thinly sliced tomatoes.

Each half serves 4.

stuffed savory meat loaf

1 pound ground beef, veal and pork mixture
½ cup dry seasoned bread crumbs
¼ cup finely chopped onion
¼ cup chopped parsley
1½ teaspoons salt
¼ teaspoon pepper
1 egg
¼ cup milk
1 cup finely diced mozzarella cheese
1 cup diced precooked ham
½ cup apricot preserves

1. In large bowl, combine ground meat mixture, bread crumbs, onion, parsley, salt, pepper, egg and milk. Mix to blend well.

2. Pat meat mixture into 10 x 8-inch oval on large sheet of damp waxed paper or plastic wrap. Mix together diced cheese and ham. Place in band down center of meat.

3. Lift up meat to enclose filling; press seams to seal well. Place seam side down on baking sheet. Bake at 350° F for 40 to 50 minutes.

4. Meanwhile, melt apricot preserves in small saucepan. Brush over meat loaf several times during last 15 minutes of cooking time. Let meat loaf stand at room temperature for 5 minutes before serving. Serve half of meat loaf immediately as an entrée.

To serve cold: Cool and chill remaining meat loaf. Cut into 8 slices; use as sandwich filling or with salad.

Each half serves 4.

meat loaf with sweet-sour sauce

3 pounds ground chuck beef
2 cups fresh bread crumbs
1 cup finely chopped onion
two 16-ounce cans tomato sauce
1 cup apricot preserves
¼ cup prepared hot mustard
¼ cup cider vinegar

1. In large mixing bowl, mix together ground beef, bread crumbs and onion; stir in 1 can of the tomato sauce and ½ cup of the apricot preserves.

2. Shape into 2 meat loaves; place side by side on 15 x 10 x 1-inch jelly-roll pan. Bake at 350° F for 50 minutes.

3. In small saucepan, combine remaining can tomato sauce, remaining apricot preserves, the mustard and vinegar. Bring to boiling point over low heat, stirring constantly.

4. Pour sauce over both meat loaves; bake 10 minutes longer. Cool 1 meat loaf for 10 minutes and serve.

DOUBLE BATCH

5. Cool second meat loaf completely in pan. Using two large spatulas, lift onto sheet of heavy-duty foil; seal tightly. Freeze up to 3 months.

6. To serve, thaw wrapped meat loaf in refrigerator overnight. Reheat wrapped meat loaf at 375° F for 20 minutes.

Each meat loaf serves 4 to 6.

potluck beef

one 16-ounce package lasagne noodles
2 tablespoons butter or margarine
2 pounds ground beef
1½ cups chopped onions
1 cup chopped green pepper
1 cup chopped celery
one 10¾-ounce can tomato soup
one 10¾-ounce can mushroom soup
one 8-ounce can tomato sauce
2 cups grated sharp Cheddar cheese
½ cup sliced green olives

1. Cook lasagne noodles according to label directions; drain, cool and cut into 1-inch pieces. Set aside.

2. Melt butter or margarine in large skillet over medium heat; add ground beef and sauté until brown, about 3 minutes. Add onions, green pepper and celery; sauté 5 minutes longer.

3. In large bowl, combine noodle pieces, tomato soup, mushroom soup, tomato sauce, 1½ cups of the cheese and the olives. Stir in meat-vegetable mixture.

4. Spoon half of mixture into lightly greased 1½-quart casserole. Line second 1½-quart casserole with foil; lightly grease and fill with remaining mixture. Sprinkle top of each with ¼ cup remaining cheese.

5. Bake both casseroles at 350° F for 40 minutes. Cool first casserole for 10 minutes before serving.

DOUBLE BATCH

6. Cool second casserole completely; cover and freeze. When completely frozen, remove food with foil lining from casserole; wrap for storing. Freeze up to 1 month.

7. To serve, unwrap and return food with foil lining to original casserole; thaw completely in refrigerator. Reheat casserole at 350° F for 20 minutes.

Each casserole serves 4.

savory meat pies

2 tablespoons butter or margarine

1½ pounds ground beef

1 clove garlic, crushed

1 teaspoon salt

½ teaspoon thyme

¼ teaspoon pepper

2 tablespoons flour

1 envelope beef powder concentrate

1 cup water

1 egg

1 tablespoon water

two 8-ounce packages refrigerator buttermilk biscuits

1. Melt butter or margarine in large skillet over low heat; add ground beef and brown for about 5 to 7 minutes, stirring constantly to break meat into small pieces.

2. Stir in garlic, salt, thyme and pepper; cook for 1 minute. Sprinkle flour and beef concentrate over beef mixture. Blend in water; bring to boiling point. Cool completely.

3. Preheat oven to 350° F.

4. Lightly beat egg with water. Roll each biscuit into 5-inch circle on lightly floured board. Place ½ cup meat mixture on each of 10 circles. Dampen all edges with a little of egg mixture. Top with remaining biscuit circles, pressing edges with fork to seal.

5. Place on two lightly greased cookie sheets; brush all pies with remaining egg mixture. Bake for 12 to 15 minutes, until golden brown. Serve half immediately.

To serve cold: Cool pies on wire rack. Wrap in plastic wrap and chill. Serve as snacks or sandwiches.

Each half serves 4.

lamb casserole

4 pounds boned leg or shoulder of lamb, cut into ¾-inch cubes

½ cup flour

1 teaspoon salt

1 teaspoon pepper

⅓ cup butter or margarine

2 cloves garlic, crushed

2 cups chicken broth

¾ cup dry sherry

3 tablespoons lemon juice

¼ cup finely chopped parsley

1. Toss lamb cubes in mixture of flour, salt and pepper to coat. Melt butter or margarine in 8-quart Dutch oven over medium heat; add lamb cubes a few at a time and sauté until well browned. Remove meat as browned and set aside.

2. Return all meat to Dutch oven. Add garlic; cook over low heat for 2 minutes, stirring constantly. Add chicken broth and sherry.

3. Cover tightly and bake at 350° F for 45 minutes or until meat is tender. Stir in lemon juice; sprinkle with parsley. Serve half of lamb casserole immediately, placing in heatproof serving dish.

DOUBLE BATCH

4. Cool remaining lamb casserole; place in freezer container and seal tightly. Freeze up to 1 month.

5. To serve, thaw, covered, in refrigerator overnight. Place in 4-quart casserole. Reheat at 350° F for 20 to 30 minutes or until piping hot.

Each half serves 4.

stuffed roast pork

two 5-pound fresh pork
    shoulders, boned
2½ cups water
one 11-ounce package mixed
    dried fruits
½ cup butter or margarine
2 cups chopped onions
½ cup chopped celery
one 16-ounce package herb-
    seasoned stuffing mix
one 16-ounce can cranberry
    sauce
½ cup orange juice
½ cup brown sugar, firmly
    packed
parsley (optional)

1. Wipe pork shoulders inside and out with damp paper towels; skin pork and set aside.

2. In large saucepan, combine water and dried fruits; simmer, covered, over low heat for 20 minutes. Let fruits cool; pit prunes and return them to saucepan. Meanwhile, melt butter or margarine in large skillet over medium heat; add onions and celery and sauté until tender, about 10 minutes, stirring constantly.

3. Add onions and celery to fruit mixture; toss in stuffing mix. Divide stuffing in half; pack one half firmly into each pork pocket. Place roasts in two separate roasting pans.

4. Roast both pork shoulders at 325° F for 2 hours. Make glaze by blending cranberry sauce, orange juice and brown sugar. Brush over both roasts; cook 1½ hours longer. Serve 1 stuffed shoulder. Garnish with parsley if desired.

DOUBLE BATCH

5. Cool second roast completely; wrap securely in heavy-duty foil. Freeze up to 1 month.

6. To serve, completely thaw foil-wrapped meat in refrigerator overnight; reheat, covered, at 350° F for 1 hour.

Each shoulder serves 6 to 8. Shown on page 66.

Note: Have a butcher remove the bone from the pork shoulder or remove it yourself with a small sharp knife.

glazed apricot ham

5- to 6-pound precooked
  smoked ham

whole cloves

one 12-ounce jar apricot
  preserves

one 8¼-ounce can crushed
  pineapple

¼ cup prepared spicy mustard

1. Trim fat from ham, leaving ¼-inch layer of fat on meat. Wipe ham well with damp paper towels. Using sharp knife, score surface into pattern of 1-inch diamonds. Place a clove in center of each diamond. Set ham in shallow roasting pan; bake at 350° F for 1 hour.

2. Meanwhile, blend apricot preserves, undrained crushed pineapple and mustard in medium saucepan over low heat. Brush meat frequently with half of glaze during last 30 minutes of cooking time.

3. Let meat stand at room temperature for 15 minutes before carving. Carve enough for 4 servings; serve remaining glaze alongside as a sauce.

To serve cold: Cool remaining meat; wrap and chill. Carve into thin slices; serve as an entrée or in salad.

Each half serves 4.

sausage bake

4 pounds hot-seasoned bulk
  sausage meat

four 1½-ounce packages
  chicken noodle soup mix

1 cup uncooked long-grain rice

8 cups water

¼ cup sausage drippings or
  vegetable oil

1 cup diced green pepper

1 cup diced celery

½ cup diced onion

½ cup slivered almonds

1. Sauté sausage meat in large skillet over low heat until well browned, about 8 to 10 minutes, stirring constantly to break meat into small pieces. Drain surplus fat from skillet, reserving ¼ cup if desired.

2. Stir soup mix and rice into sausage meat in skillet; blend in water. Bring mixture to boiling point over medium heat. Reduce heat to low and simmer, covered, for 10 minutes, stirring occasionally.

3. Pour reserved sausage drippings or oil into medium skillet; add green pepper, celery and onion and sauté over medium heat until tender, about 5 minutes. Add to sausage mixture.

4. Spoon half of mixture into lightly greased 2-quart casserole. Line second 2-quart casserole with foil; lightly grease and fill with remaining sausage mixture. Sprinkle ¼ cup slivered almonds over each.

5. Bake both casseroles at 325° F for 30 minutes. Cool first casserole for 10 minutes, then serve.

DOUBLE BATCH

6. Cool second casserole completely; cover and freeze. When completely frozen, remove food with foil lining from casserole; wrap for storing. Freeze up to 1 month.

7. To serve, unwrap and return food with foil lining to original casserole; cover and thaw completely in refrigerator. Uncover and reheat at 350° F for 20 minutes.

Each casserole serves 4.

sausage loaf

1 pound seasoned bulk sausage meat
1 cup chopped celery
½ cup chopped onion
3 cups diced day-old white bread
¼ cup chopped parsley
1 envelope chicken powder concentrate
½ teaspoon poultry seasoning
¼ teaspoon pepper
1 egg, beaten
¾ cup milk

1. Brown sausage meat in large skillet over medium heat for about 10 minutes, stirring constantly to break meat into small pieces. Remove from skillet with slotted spoon; place in large bowl.

2. Pour all but 2 tablespoons drippings from skillet; add celery and onion to drippings in skillet and sauté until tender, about 5 minutes, stirring constantly. Add to sausage meat in bowl.

3. Stir in bread, parsley, chicken concentrate, poultry seasoning and pepper. Stir in beaten egg and milk. Spoon mixture into lightly greased 9 x 5 x 3-inch loaf pan.

4. Bake at 350° F for 35 minutes or until lightly browned. Let stand at room temperature for 5 minutes before serving. Serve half of loaf as an entrée.

To serve cold: Cool and chill remaining meat loaf. Remove from pan; cut into 8 slices and use as sandwich filling or with salad.

Each half serves 4.

crispy fried chicken

two 3-pound broiler-fryer
  chickens, cut into serving
  pieces
½ cup unflavored yogurt
2 teaspoons paprika
2 cups packaged crushed herb
  stuffing mix
½ cup grated Parmesan cheese
1 cup butter or margarine,
  melted

1. Wash chicken pieces under cold running water; pat dry with paper towels. In large bowl, blend together yogurt and paprika; add chicken pieces, tossing to coat well.

2. In large, clean plastic or brown paper bag, mix crushed stuffing mix with grated cheese. Place chicken pieces a few at a time in bag; shake to coat well.

3. Divide chicken between two lightly greased, large shallow baking pans; drizzle with melted butter or margarine and bake at 400° F for 45 minutes. Serve one pan of chicken pieces immediately.

DOUBLE BATCH

4. Cool chicken in pan to room temperature; place in freezer. When pieces are solidly frozen, place chicken in freezer bag and seal tightly, pressing out all air. Store up to 2 months.

5. To serve, remove chicken from bag and place in shallow baking pan; cover and thaw completely in refrigerator overnight. Uncover and reheat at 400° F for 25 to 30 minutes.

Each half serves 4 to 6.

oven-fried chicken

two 2- to 2½-pound broiler-fryer
  chickens, cut into serving
  pieces
1 cup all-purpose flour
¼ cup dried parsley
1 tablespoon paprika
1 teaspoon salt
½ teaspoon pepper
⅔ cup vegetable oil

1. Wash chicken pieces well under cold running water; pat dry with paper towels. In large, clean brown paper or plastic bag, combine flour, parsley, salt and pepper. Place chicken pieces two at a time in bag; shake to coat well.

2. Pour oil into large roasting pan; heat in oven for 10 minutes. Place chicken pieces in hot oil; bake at 400° F for 40 minutes, turning once or twice to cook evenly, until golden brown and tender. Serve half of chicken hot.

To serve cold: Remove chicken from roasting pan; cool and chill. Serve with potato salad.

Each half serves 4.

chicken parmesan

8 chicken breast halves, boned

2 eggs, slightly beaten

1 cup dry seasoned bread crumbs

¼ cup grated Parmesan cheese

¼ cup vegetable oil

½ pound mozzarella cheese, cut into 8 slices

one 15½-ounce jar spaghetti sauce

1. Wash chicken well under cold running water; pat dry with paper towels. Place each chicken breast between two sheets of waxed paper; using wooden mallet or rolling pin, pound to flatten evenly.

2. Pour slightly beaten eggs onto one plate; mix bread crumbs and Parmesan cheese and place on second plate. Dip chicken breasts in beaten egg to coat; drain slightly and dip in bread crumbs to coat. Chill for 30 minutes to seal coating.

3. Heat 2 tablespoons of the oil in large skillet over medium heat; add chicken breast halves four at a time and sauté until crisp and tender, about 2 to 3 minutes per side. Add remaining oil as necessary. Remove chicken as browned and set aside.

4. Arrange chicken breasts and mozzarella cheese slices alternately in overlapping lines in 13 x 9 x 2-inch baking dish. Pour spaghetti sauce over chicken; let stand for 5 minutes. Bake at 350° F for 20 minutes; serve half immediately as an entrée.

To serve cold: Cool and chill remaining chicken. Serve as sandwich filling in crusty hero rolls or as a salad.

Each half serves 4.

chicken salad casserole

1 pound precooked chicken roll, diced, or 4 cups diced cooked chicken

2 cups diced celery

½ cup chopped onion

1 cup mayonnaise

1 cup sour cream

¼ cup lemon juice

1 teaspoon salt

½ teaspoon pepper

potato chips

lettuce leaves

1. In large bowl, combine chicken, celery, onion, mayonnaise, sour cream, lemon juice, salt and pepper.

2. Spoon half of mixture into 1-quart casserole; top with 1 cup crushed potato chips. Bake at 375° F for 20 to 30 minutes or until very hot.

To serve cold: Line salad bowl with lettuce leaves. Spoon in remaining chicken salad. Chill; serve with whole potato chips.

Each half serves 4.

tuna quiche

one 9- to 11-ounce package
  piecrust mix

three 7-ounce cans water-
  packed tuna

½ cup chopped green onions

10 eggs

3 cups half-and-half or
  evaporated milk

½ cup grated Swiss cheese

1 teaspoon dry mustard

1 teaspoon salt

½ teaspoon pepper

paprika

1. Prepare piecrust mix according to label directions. Roll out to line two 9-inch pie plates. Trim and flute edges of pastry; prick pastry shells with fork.

2. Preheat oven to 350° F.

3. Drain and flake tuna; spread half over bottom of each pastry shell. Sprinkle each portion with ¼ cup green onion.

4. In large bowl, beat together eggs and half-and-half or evaporated milk; stir in cheese, dry mustard, salt and pepper. Divide egg mixture between pastry shells. Sprinkle with paprika.

5. Bake quiches for 40 to 50 minutes or until knife inserted in center comes out clean. Cool 1 quiche for 10 minutes before serving.

DOUBLE BATCH

6. Cool second quiche completely; wrap tightly in heavy-duty foil. Freeze up to 1 month.

7. To serve, preheat oven to 400° F. Place frozen quiche in oven and immediately reduce temperature to 350° F. Cook for 10 minutes.

Each quiche serves 6.

shrimp-stuffed potatoes

8 large baking potatoes

two 10¾-ounce cans cream of
  shrimp soup

¼ cup butter or margarine

¼ cup chopped parsley

2 tablespoons lemon juice

1. Wash potatoes and prick all over with fork. Bake at 450° F for 45 to 60 minutes, depending on size, until easily pierced with a skewer.

2. Cut ½-inch slice from top of each potato; carefully scoop out pulp into large bowl.

3. Using electric mixer at medium speed, beat together potato pulp, shrimp soup, butter or margarine, parsley and lemon juice. Fill potato shells with shrimp mixture.

4. Return potatoes to oven; reheat for 20 minutes. Serve 4 stuffed potatoes immediately.

DOUBLE BATCH

5. Cool remaining potatoes completely; wrap individually in foil. Freeze up to 2 months.

6. To serve, thaw wrapped potatoes in refrigerator; reheat at 350° F for 20 minutes.

Each half serves 4.

sesame-salmon turnovers

two 3¾-ounce cans salmon, drained, boned and flaked

one 3-ounce package cream cheese

1 egg, separated

2 tablespoons chopped stuffed olives

1 tablespoon mayonnaise

2 teaspoons instant minced onion

1 teaspoon dried dill

¼ teaspoon pepper

six 8-ounce packages refrigerator crescent rolls

2 tablespoons water

½ cup sesame seeds

1. In medium bowl, combine flaked salmon, cream cheese, egg yolk, olives, mayonnaise, minced onion, dill and pepper. Blend well.

2. Open 1 package refrigerator crescent rolls; unroll half of dough at a time onto lightly floured board, pressing lightly to seal perforations and form 1 piece. Roll into 15 x 6-inch rectangle. Cut into 2-inch circles. Repeat, using second half of dough.

3. Lightly beat together egg white and water. Place ½ teaspoon salmon filling in center of each circle; brush edges of dough with a little of egg white-water mixture. Fold dough over filling; press edges together with fork to seal. Repeat, using remaining dough and filling.

4. Preheat oven to 400° F.

5. Brush turnovers with remaining egg white-water mixture; sprinkle with sesame seeds. Place on baking sheets; bake for 10 minutes or until golden brown. Serve warm as hors d'oeuvres.

DOUBLE BATCH

6. Cool 5 dozen turnovers completely. Seal in plastic containers or wrap in heavy-duty foil. Freeze up to 3 months.

7. To serve, unwrap and place, frozen, on baking sheets in 425° F oven for 5 to 7 minutes or until piping hot.

Makes 10 dozen hors d'oeuvres.

spinach pie

one 9- to 11-ounce package
  piecrust mix
two 10-ounce packages frozen
  chopped spinach
½ cup butter or margarine
1 teaspoon nutmeg
½ teaspoon pepper
one 16-ounce container small
  curd cottage cheese
6 eggs, slightly beaten
1 cup grated Parmesan cheese
1 cup half-and-half or
  evaporated milk

1. Prepare piecrust mix according to label directions. Roll out to line two 9-inch pie plates. Trim and flute edges of pastry; prick pastry shells with fork.

2. Preheat oven to 350° F.

3. Cook spinach according to label directions; drain well. Beat in butter or margarine, nutmeg and pepper.

4. In large bowl, blend cottage cheese, slightly beaten eggs, Parmesan cheese and half-and-half or evaporated milk. Stir in spinach mixture, blending well. Divide mixture between pastry shells.

5. Bake for 40 to 50 minutes or until knife inserted in center comes out clean. Cool 1 Spinach Pie for 10 minutes before serving.

DOUBLE BATCH

6. Cool second pie completely; wrap tightly in heavy-duty foil. Freeze up to 1 month.

7. To serve, preheat oven to 400° F. Place frozen pie in oven and immediately reduce heat to 350° F. Cook for 10 minutes.

Each pie serves 6.

elegant artichoke bake

two 14-ounce cans artichoke
  hearts, drained
2 cups mayonnaise
½ cup grated Parmesan cheese
1 clove garlic, crushed
½ teaspoon pepper

1. Coarsely chop drained artichokes. Place in medium bowl; blend in mayonnaise, grated cheese, garlic and pepper.

2. Divide mixture among eight 6-ounce ovenproof custard cups or individual soufflé dishes. Bake at 350° F for 15 minutes. Serve 4 portions immediately as a vegetable.

To serve cold: Cool and chill remaining 4 portions. Serve as hors d'oeuvres or unmold and serve as part of salad.

Each half serves 4.

carrot casserole

2 pounds carrots

two 10¾-ounce cans cream of celery soup

2 cups grated sharp Cheddar cheese

½ cup dry unseasoned bread crumbs

2 tablespoons butter or margarine, melted

1. Peel carrots and cut into julienne strips to measure 6 cups. Place in boiling salted water in medium saucepan; cook over medium heat until tender, about 15 minutes. Drain.

2. Add celery soup and grated cheese to carrots; gently mix. Spoon half of mixture into lightly greased 1½-quart casserole. Line second 1½-quart casserole with foil; lightly grease and fill with remaining mixture.

3. Blend together bread crumbs and melted butter or margarine; sprinkle top of each casserole with ¼ cup of mixture. Bake both casseroles at 350° F for 20 minutes; serve first casserole immediately.

DOUBLE BATCH

4. Cool second casserole completely; cover and freeze. When completely frozen, remove food with foil lining from casserole; wrap for storing. Freeze up to 1 month.

5. To serve, return food with foil lining to original casserole; thaw completely in refrigerator. Reheat at 375° F for 15 minutes.

Each casserole serves 4.

creamy potato puff

4 cups instant mashed potatoes

two 8-ounce packages cream cheese

2 eggs, beaten

½ cup finely chopped onion

½ cup finely chopped pimiento

½ cup finely chopped parsley

1 teaspoon salt

1. Prepare instant mashed potatoes to yield 12 servings. Beat cream cheese into hot potatoes until thoroughly blended.

2. Beat in beaten eggs, onion, pimiento, parsley and salt. Divide mixture between two 1-quart casseroles. Bake both casseroles at 350° F for 45 minutes; serve one immediately.

DOUBLE BATCH

3. Cool second Creamy Potato Puff completely; wrap casserole tightly in heavy-duty foil; freeze up to 1 month.

4. To serve, place wrapped casserole in refrigerator for 2 to 3 hours, until thawed. Reheat at 375° F for 20 minutes or until piping hot.

Each casserole serves 4.

eggplant casserole

½ cup butter or margarine

one 2-pound eggplant, peeled
  and cubed

2 cups chopped celery

1 cup chopped onion

1 cup chopped green pepper

one 16-ounce can tomato
  sauce

2 cups shredded sharp Cheddar
  cheese

2 cups coarsely crushed corn
  chips

1. Melt butter or margarine in large skillet over medium heat; add eggplant, celery, onion and green pepper and sauté until tender, about 15 minutes, stirring constantly. Stir in tomato sauce, shredded cheese and ½ cup of the crushed corn chips.

2. Spoon half of mixture into lightly greased 1½-quart casserole. Cover and bake at 325° F for 30 minutes; remove cover and sprinkle top of casserole with ¾ cup of the crushed corn chips. Switch off oven and let casserole continue cooking 10 minutes longer.

DOUBLE BATCH

3. Spoon remaining mixture into second lightly greased 1½-quart foil-lined casserole. Cover and freeze without baking.

4. When frozen, remove food with foil lining from casserole; wrap for storing, taping small container of remaining ¾ cup corn chips to food. Freeze up to 3 months.

5. To serve, unwrap and return food with foil lining to original casserole; thaw completely. Bake as above.

Each casserole serves 4.

eggplant italian

1½- to 2-pound eggplant

3 eggs, slightly beaten

1¼ cups dry seasoned bread
  crumbs

¼ cup grated Parmesan cheese

2 tablespoons vegetable oil

1½ teaspoons salt

½ teaspoon pepper

½ pound mozzarella cheese,
  cut into ¼-inch-thick slices

one 15½-ounce jar spaghetti
  sauce

one 8-ounce can tomato sauce

1. Wash eggplant; dry with paper towels. Cut crosswise into ⅓-inch-thick slices. Pour slightly beaten eggs into 9-inch pie plate; combine bread crumbs and Parmesan cheese in second pie plate.

2. Dip eggplant slices into beaten eggs to coat; drain slightly and dip into bread crumbs to coat. Place on baking sheet in single layer; chill to seal coating.

3. Heat oil in large skillet over medium heat; add eggplant slices a few at a time and fry until brown and crisp, about 2 minutes per side. Add more oil if necessary. Remove slices as browned and drain on paper towels; sprinkle each slice with a little salt and pepper.

4. Arrange eggplant slices and mozzarella cheese slices alternately in overlapping lines in 13 x 9 x 2-inch baking dish. Mix together spa-

ghetti sauce and tomato sauce. Pour over eggplant; let stand for 5 minutes. Bake at 350° F for 30 minutes; serve half as an entrée.

To serve cold: Cool and chill remaining eggplant. Serve as filling for hard crusty rolls, dressed with a little oil and vinegar.

Each half serves 4.

home-style white bread

12 to 13 cups all-purpose flour
4 packages dry yeast
¾ cup nonfat dry milk powder
⅓ cup sugar
1 tablespoon salt
4 cups water
¼ cup butter or margarine

1. In large bowl, stir together 5 cups of the flour, the yeast, dry milk powder, sugar and salt. Heat water and butter or margarine in medium saucepan over low heat until water is warm and butter is melted. (Take care water is not too hot; it should be just comfortable when felt with finger—about 120° F.)

2. Using electric mixer at low speed, gradually add water and butter to dry ingredients; beat mixture until smooth. Add another 2 cups flour; beat until smooth.

3. Using electric mixer, or by hand, blend in enough additional flour to make a stiff dough; dough should leave sides of bowl.

4. Turn dough onto lightly floured board; knead until smooth and elastic. Divide dough into 4 equal pieces. Knead and shape 1 piece to fit well-greased 9 x 5 x 3-inch loaf pan.

5. Let rise until double in bulk; preheat oven to 350° F.

6. Bake for 35 minutes, until bread is golden brown and sounds hollow when tapped. Remove from pan and cool on wire rack.

DOUBLE BATCH

7. Shape remaining 3 pieces of dough into round balls. Cover with plastic wrap; set on baking sheet and freeze. When completely frozen, remove plastic wrap; rewrap in foil. Freeze up to 1 month.

8. To serve, unwrap and let stand at room temperature until completely thawed, about 4 hours, or place in refrigerator overnight. Shape into loaves; set in prepared pans. Let rise, bake and cool as directed above.

Makes 4 loaves

zucchini nut bread

4 eggs
2 cups sugar
1 cup vegetable oil
3½ cups all-purpose flour
1½ teaspoons baking soda
1½ teaspoons cinnamon
1 teaspoon baking powder
1 teaspoon salt
½ teaspoon nutmeg
½ teaspoon ginger
2 cups grated unpared zucchini
1 cup chopped walnuts
1 cup golden raisins
2 teaspoons vanilla extract

1. Preheat oven to 350° F.

2. Using electric mixer at high speed, beat eggs in large bowl until light and foamy; gradually add sugar, beating until thick and lemon colored. Beat in oil.

3. In separate bowl, combine flour, baking soda, cinnamon, baking powder, salt, nutmeg and ginger. Using mixer at low speed, alternately add dry ingredients and zucchini to egg mixture. Blend mixture thoroughly.

4. Stir in walnuts, raisins and vanilla extract. Divide mixture between two greased and floured 9 x 5 x 3-inch loaf pans.

5. Bake for 55 to 60 minutes or until toothpick inserted in center comes out clean. Cool bread in pans on wire rack for 10 minutes. Remove from pans; cool completely.

DOUBLE BATCH

6. Wrap 1 loaf tightly in heavy-duty foil. Freeze up to 1 month. Thaw at room temperature for 30 minutes before serving.

Makes 2 loaves.

OVEN MEALS

VEAL BIRDS MENU

OVEN MANAGEMENT: *Preheat oven to 375° F.* Bake Glazed Acorn Squash, placing on shelf set in bottom third of oven. Make Irish Soda Bread; place on shelf set in top third of oven. Make Veal Birds; set on higher shelf, moving Irish Soda Bread to lower shelf beside Glazed Acorn Squash. *Menu shown on front cover.*

glazed acorn squash

2 medium acorn squash
½ cup water
⅓ cup butter or margarine
⅓ cup dark corn syrup
⅓ cup chopped walnuts
½ teaspoon grated lemon rind
¼ teaspoon cinnamon

1. Cut squash in half; using teaspoon, scoop out seeds and stringy pulp. Place cut side down in greased shallow baking pan; add water to pan. Bake for 30 minutes.

2. In small saucepan, combine butter or margarine, corn syrup, walnuts, lemon rind and cinnamon. Heat over low heat to melt butter or margarine; stir to mix well.

3. Turn squash cut side up; spoon one-fourth of mixture into each squash half. Bake 20 minutes longer.

Serves 4.

irish soda bread

4 cups all-purpose flour
¼ cup sugar
1 teaspoon salt
1 teaspoon baking powder
¼ cup butter or margarine
2 cups golden raisins
1 tablespoon caraway seeds
1⅓ cups buttermilk
1 egg
1 teaspoon baking soda
1 tablespoon butter or margarine, melted

1. In large bowl, sift together flour, sugar, salt and baking powder; using two knives or a pastry blender, cut ¼ cup butter or margarine into dry ingredients until mixture resembles coarse cornmeal. Stir in raisins and caraway seeds.

2. In small bowl, beat together buttermilk, egg and baking soda. Stir into dry ingredients just until moistened. Turn mixture into generously greased round 1-quart casserole; using sharp knife, cut cross in top of dough.

3. Bake for 50 minutes, or until top is crisp and brown and bread sounds hollow when tapped. Remove from casserole to wire rack; brush top with 1 tablespoon melted butter or margarine. Serve warm.

Makes 1 loaf.

veal birds

4 veal cutlets

¼ cup butter or margarine, melted

½ cup crushed cornflakes

4 slices Swiss cheese

one 10¾-ounce can cream of mushroom soup

½ cup dry white wine

1. Wipe veal cutlets with damp paper towels. Brush both sides of each cutlet with melted butter or margarine; dip in cornflakes to coat.

2. Place cheese slice on top of each cutlet; roll up each cutlet jelly-roll fashion and secure with toothpicks. Place seam side down in lightly greased 8 x 8 x 2-inch baking dish.

3. Combine mushroom soup with wine; pour around veal rolls. Bake for 40 minutes.

Serves 4.

HAM LOAVES MENU

OVEN MANAGEMENT: *Preheat oven to 375° F.* Arrange two shelves to divide oven into thirds. Assemble Individual Ham Loaves, Sweet Potato Puffs and Green Bean Casserole. Place all three in oven together, setting Individual Ham Loaves and Green Bean Casserole side by side on lower shelf and Sweet Potato Puffs on higher shelf.

individual ham loaves

one 8-ounce can pineapple rings

2 cups ground precooked ham

½ cup dry seasoned bread crumbs

2 tablespoons brown sugar

1 tablespoon mint jelly

½ teaspoon ground cloves

1. Drain pineapple rings, reserving ½ cup juice. Place rings in bottom of lightly greased 8 x 8 x 2-inch baking dish.

2. In medium bowl, combine ground ham, bread crumbs, brown sugar, mint jelly and cloves. Stir in reserved pineapple juice.

3. Shape mixture into 4 individual round loaves the same diameter as pineapple rings. Place one on each ring. Bake for 25 minutes or until loaves are hot and golden.

Serves 4.

sweet potato puffs

two 16-ounce cans vacuum-packed sweet potatoes

two 8-ounce cans crushed pineapple, drained

2 eggs

¼ cup brown sugar, firmly packed

¼ cup butter or margarine, melted

2 teaspoons grated lemon rind

½ teaspoon ground cloves

½ teaspoon nutmeg

1. Using electric mixer at medium speed, beat together sweet potatoes and drained pineapple in large bowl. Beat in eggs, brown sugar and melted butter or margarine until light and fluffy; beat in lemon rind, cloves and nutmeg.

2. Drop mixture in 8 mounds on lightly greased baking sheet. Bake for 25 minutes or until golden.

Serves 4.

green bean casserole

two 10-ounce packages frozen French-style green beans

2 tablespoons flour

2 tablespoons butter or margarine

1 cup sour cream

½ teaspoon salt

½ teaspoon sugar

½ cup diced Swiss cheese

¼ cup grated Parmesan cheese

1. Place green beans briefly under running water to thaw. Drain well; set aside.

2. In small saucepan, heat flour and butter or margarine until butter or margarine is melted and mixture is bubbling. Remove from heat; whisk in sour cream, salt and sugar.

3. Stir green beans into sour cream mixture. Spoon into lightly greased 1-quart casserole. Top with mixture of diced Swiss cheese and grated Parmesan cheese. Cover and bake for 25 minutes; uncover and bake 5 minutes longer.

Serves 4.

EnergySaving Tip: To thaw frozen vegetables quickly, take them out of the package and place the frozen vegetable block in a sieve under cold running water for a minute or two. Let frozen fruits stand in the package in warm water for 15 to 20 minutes. The fastest way to thaw both vegetables and fruits is to place them, unwrapped, in a microwave oven for 1 minute on the thaw cycle. Thawing saves cooking time, and less cooking time means less energy is used.

CHICKEN CASSEROLE MENU

OVEN MANAGEMENT: *Preheat oven to 350° F.* Make Chicken Casserole, placing on shelf set in bottom third of oven. Make Cranberry Nut Bread, placing on shelf set in top third of oven. Make Baked Peach Halves; place on lower oven shelf. Uncover Chicken Casserole and place on top shelf to brown; at the same time move Cranberry Nut Bread to lower shelf beside peaches.

chicken casserole

2½- to 3-pound broiler-fryer chicken, cut into serving pieces

⅓ cup mayonnaise

2 teaspoons paprika

1 cup uncooked long-grain rice

one 1.38-ounce package onion soup mix

1 cup beef broth

¾ cup water

one 4-ounce can sliced mushrooms

1. Wash chicken pieces under cold running water; pat dry with paper towels. Brush all sides of chicken with mayonnaise and sprinkle with paprika; set aside.

2. In lightly greased 2-quart casserole, combine rice, onion soup mix, beef broth, water and undrained mushrooms. Place chicken on top. Cover tightly.

3. Bake for 45 minutes. Uncover and bake 15 minutes longer or until chicken is golden brown.

Serves 4.

cranberry nut bread

2 cups all-purpose flour

1 cup sugar

1½ teaspoons baking powder

1 teaspoon salt

½ teaspoon baking soda

¼ cup butter, margarine or vegetable shortening

¾ cup orange juice

1 egg

1 teaspoon grated orange rind

¾ cup chopped fresh cranberries

½ cup chopped walnuts

1. In large bowl, sift together flour, sugar, baking powder, salt and baking soda; using two knives or a pastry blender, cut shortening into dry ingredients until mixture resembles coarse crumbs.

2. In small bowl, beat together orange juice, egg and orange rind. Stir into dry ingredients just until moistened; fold in cranberries and walnuts.

3. Pour batter into generously greased 9 x 5 x 3-inch loaf pan. Bake for 1 hour or until toothpick inserted in center comes out clean.

Makes 1 loaf.

baked peach halves

one 16-ounce can cling peach halves, drained

¾ cup prepared mincemeat

½ cup chopped walnuts or pecans

¼ cup dark rum or orange juice

½ cup heavy cream

2 tablespoons confectioners' sugar

1. Place drained cling peach halves cut side up in lightly greased 8 x 8 x 2-inch baking dish.

2. In small bowl, blend mincemeat, chopped nuts and rum or orange juice. Fill centers of peach halves with mixture. Bake for 15 minutes.

3. Using electric mixer at high speed, beat cream in small bowl until stiff; beat in confectioners' sugar. Swirl whipped cream over peaches just before serving.

Serves 4.

CREAMY RICE AND CHICKEN MENU

OVEN MANAGEMENT: *Preheat oven to 350° F.* Arrange two shelves to divide oven into thirds. Make Carrot Ring; place on lower shelf. Make Creamy Rice and Chicken; place on shelf next to carrots. Make Ginger-Baked Bananas; place on higher shelf.

carrot ring

1 pound carrots

1 cup fresh bread crumbs

¼ cup chopped parsley

¼ cup grated onion

1 teaspoon salt

¼ teaspoon nutmeg

2 eggs

½ cup evaporated milk or half-and-half

¼ cup butter or margarine, melted

1. Peel carrots and cut into thin slices; place in medium saucepan with 1 inch salted water. Bring to boiling point; reduce heat to low and simmer, covered, until tender, about 10 minutes. Drain carrots and mash finely.

2. In large bowl, combine mashed carrots, bread crumbs, parsley, onion, salt and nutmeg. Beat in eggs, evaporated milk or half-and-half, and melted butter or margarine.

3. Pour mixture into well-greased 4-quart ring mold. Bake for 45 minutes or until knife inserted in center comes out clean. Let stand for 10 minutes at room temperature; unmold on serving platter.

Serves 4.

creamy rice and chicken

1 cup uncooked long-grain rice

2 cups diced cooked chicken, or 1 pound precooked chicken roll, diced

¼ cup finely chopped pimiento

one 10¾-ounce can cream of celery soup

½ cup dry sherry

¼ cup dry unseasoned bread crumbs

2 tablespoons butter or margarine, melted

1. Cook rice according to label directions. Place in large bowl; combine with chicken, pimiento, celery soup and sherry.

2. Spoon mixture into lightly greased 1½-quart casserole; top with mixture of bread crumbs and melted butter or margarine.

3. Bake for 30 minutes. Serve alongside Carrot Ring or spoon into center of ring.

Serves 4.

ginger-baked bananas

4 medium bananas, slightly firm

1 cup brown sugar, firmly packed

¼ cup orange juice

¼ cup lemon juice or white rum

¼ cup chopped crystallized ginger

1. Peel bananas; cut lengthwise in half. Place cut side down in lightly greased 9 x 9 x 2-inch baking dish.

2. In small bowl, mix together brown sugar, orange juice and lemon juice or rum. Spoon some of mixture over each banana. Sprinkle with chopped ginger. Bake for 20 minutes or until tender; spoon cooking liquid over bananas before serving.

Serves 4.

EnergySaving Tip: Don't preheat the oven when you're roasting meats, baking fruit or cooking vegetable, meat, pasta, rice or bean casseroles—it's an unnecessary energy drain. Preheat only when a recipe advises it: for baked goods that need to rise, like breads and cakes made with yeast or baking powder; pies, pie shells, cookies and pastries; delicate dishes that include separated eggs, like soufflés and meringues; custards and quiches in which eggs must be set. The baking times in this book take into account this energy-saving practice.

CRABMEAT STRATA MENU

Preheat oven to 350° F. Bake Crabmeat Strata on shelf set in top third of oven. Make Baked Tomatoes and place on shelf set in bottom third of oven.

crabmeat strata

2 cups fresh bread crumbs

one 6-ounce package frozen crabmeat, thawed and drained

¼ cup mayonnaise

¼ cup finely sliced green onion

¼ cup finely chopped pimiento

2 tablespoons chopped parsley

2 teaspoons prepared spicy mustard

½ cup grated mild Cheddar cheese

2 eggs

1 cup milk

1. Generously grease 1-quart casserole; cover bottom with bread crumbs. Set aside.

2. Flake crabmeat into medium bowl; stir in mayonnaise, green onion, pimiento, parsley and mustard. Spread mixture over crumbs. Sprinkle with grated cheese.

3. In small bowl, beat together eggs and milk. Pour over casserole; let stand for 5 minutes. Cover casserole with foil. Bake for 30 minutes; remove foil and bake 5 to 10 minutes longer or until top is golden brown. Serve immediately.

Serves 4.

baked tomatoes

2 large tomatoes

⅓ cup dry seasoned bread crumbs

2 tablespoons grated sharp Cheddar cheese

1 tablespoon mayonnaise

1 tablespoon sour cream

1. Cut tomatoes in half. Using small, sharp knife, make 3 or 4 deep cuts in center of each half. Place tomatoes in well-greased, small shallow baking dish.

2. In small bowl, combine bread crumbs, grated cheese, mayonnaise and sour cream. Divide mixture among tomatoes, spreading over top of each. Bake for 20 minutes.

Serves 4.

TUNA-EGG CASSEROLE MENU

OVEN MANAGEMENT: *Preheat oven to 400° F.* Arrange two shelves to divide oven into thirds. Make Snickerdoodles, using both shelves to bake cookies. Make Tuna-Egg Casserole, placing on lower shelf. Make Graham Muffins, placing on higher oven shelf.

snickerdoodles

2¾ cups all-purpose flour
2 teaspoons cream of tartar
1 teaspoon baking powder
½ teaspoon salt
1¼ cups sugar
1 cup butter, margarine or vegetable shortening
2 eggs
2 tablespoons sugar
2 teaspoons cinnamon

1. In medium bowl, sift together flour, cream of tartar, baking powder and salt; set aside.

2. Using electric mixer at medium speed, beat together 1¼ cups sugar and the shortening in large bowl until creamy. Beat in eggs. With mixer at low speed, blend in flour mixture. Chill dough for at least 15 minutes or until ready to bake.

3. Roll dough into walnut-size balls; roll each in mixture of 2 tablespoons sugar and the cinnamon to coat. Place 2 inches apart on lightly greased cookie sheet. Bake cookies for 8 to 10 minutes or until lightly browned.

Makes approximately 4 dozen cookies.

tuna-egg casserole

one 7-ounce can oil-packed tuna, drained
2 hard-cooked eggs, chopped
one 10-ounce package frozen mixed vegetables, thawed and drained
one 10¾-ounce can cream of celery soup
1 tablespoon lemon juice
¼ teaspoon pepper
¾ cup crushed potato chips

1. Flake drained tuna into large bowl with fork; add chopped eggs. Stir in mixed vegetables. Blend in celery soup, lemon juice and pepper.

2. Spoon mixture into lightly greased 1½-quart casserole. Top with potato chips. Bake for 30 minutes or until brown and bubbling.

Serves 4.

graham muffins

1½ cups graham flour
3 tablespoons sugar
1 teaspoon baking soda
½ teaspoon salt
1 cup buttermilk
3 tablespoons molasses

1. In large bowl, sift together graham flour, sugar, baking soda and salt. In small bowl, beat together buttermilk and molasses.

2. Stir liquid into dry ingredients just until moistened. Pour mixture into six lightly greased 2½-inch muffin cups, filling two-thirds full. Bake for 25 minutes.

Makes 6 muffins.

EGGPLANT ROLLS MENU

OVEN MANAGEMENT: *Preheat oven to 375° F.* Make Eggplant Rolls, placing on shelf set in top third of oven. Make Spumoni Cookies; set on upper shelf, moving Eggplant Rolls to shelf set in bottom third of oven. Make Garlic Bread; place beside Eggplant Rolls.

eggplant rolls

1 medium eggplant
one 16-ounce container ricotta or small curd cottage cheese
2 cups grated mozzarella cheese
½ cup grated Parmesan cheese
¼ cup chopped parsley
1 egg, beaten
1 tablespoon lemon juice
1 egg
1 tablespoon water
1 cup dry seasoned bread crumbs
¼ cup butter or margarine
two 8-ounce cans tomato sauce

1. Wash eggplant under cold running water; dry and cut lengthwise into ¼-inch slices. (There will be 8 to 10 slices.) Bring 2 inches salted water to boiling point in large saucepan over medium heat. Plunge eggplant slices into boiling water; cook just until soft and pliable enough to roll, about 2 minutes. Drain eggplant on paper towels and pat dry.

2. In medium bowl, combine ricotta or cottage cheese, mozzarella cheese, ¼ cup of the Parmesan cheese, the parsley, beaten egg and lemon juice. Spread mixture over eggplant slices. Roll up slices jelly-roll fashion; secure with toothpicks.

3. Beat together egg and water; pour onto plate. Blend together bread crumbs and remaining ¼ cup Parmesan cheese; place on second plate. Dip eggplant rolls into egg mixture; drain slightly. Roll in bread crumb mixture to coat well.

4. Melt butter or margarine in large skillet over medium heat; add eggplant rolls and sauté for about 5 minutes, turning to brown all sides. Place in 9 x 9 x 2-inch baking dish. Pour tomato sauce around rolls; bake for 30 minutes.

Serves 4.

spumoni cookies

2 cups all-purpose flour

½ teaspoon baking soda

½ cup butter, margarine or vegetable shortening

1 cup brown sugar, firmly packed

¾ cup buttermilk

1 egg

¾ cup finely snipped dates

½ cup chopped almonds

¼ cup chopped candied citrus peel

¼ cup chopped candied lemon peel

¼ cup chopped candied cherries

1. In small bowl, sift together flour and baking soda; set aside.

2. Using electric mixer at medium speed, beat together shortening and brown sugar in large bowl until creamy. Beat in buttermilk and egg. With mixer at low speed, blend in flour mixture; then blend in dates, almonds, citrus peel, lemon peel and cherries.

3. Drop dough by teaspoonfuls onto lightly greased cookie sheet, 2 inches apart. (Keep unused dough chilled until baking time.) Bake for 8 to 10 minutes, until golden brown.

Makes approximately 4 dozen cookies.

garlic bread

1 loaf crusty Italian or French bread

½ cup butter or margarine, softened

2 tablespoons grated Parmesan cheese

2 cloves garlic, crushed

¼ teaspoon sage

1. Cut bread diagonally into ½-inch slices, cutting to within ¼ inch of bottom crust.

2. In small bowl, beat together butter or margarine, grated cheese, garlic and sage. Spread mixture on cut sides of all slices.

3. Wrap bread tightly in foil; bake for 15 minutes.

Serves 4.

toaster oven

What portable appliance can grill, brown, bake, broil and toast; easily prepare a midnight snack for one or a main course for four? If you answered "toaster oven," you win, because you already appreciate the versatility of this wonderful little convenience. If you didn't know the answer, you need to be filled in on the many-faceted toaster oven.

Though usually thought of as a handy counter-top appliance for the small family or single person, the toaster oven is ideal for any size household. It's a pennywise energy source that can broil hearty Beef and Cheese Heroes, bake a scrumptious Cheese and Spinach Strata for four or grill crunchy Shrimp Toast Canapés for elegant entertaining. And since it heats only the food and not the whole kitchen, it can help cut down on expensive summertime air conditioning. Best of all, toaster ovens are equipped with glass doors so you can see your creations bubble and brown to perfection right before your eyes—without letting any precious heat escape. Don't worry that your stock of pans won't fit into these compact appliances. Besides accommodating single-portion baking dishes, toaster ovens can easily handle generous 8 x 4 x 2½-inch heatproof glass loaf pans and 9 x 5 x 3-inch metal pans.

Plunge ahead and discover exciting, new mouth-watering recipes that make the most of this wonderfully versatile and convenient appliance.

puffy cheese hors d'oeuvres

4 slices white bread
2 slices bacon
½ cup finely chopped onion
2 eggs, separated
½ teaspoon salt
⅛ teaspoon pepper
1 cup grated Swiss cheese

1. Trim crusts from bread. Lightly toast each slice in toaster oven; cut each into 4 squares and set aside.

2. Fry bacon in medium skillet over low heat until crisp. Drain on paper towel; crumble and set aside.

3. Pour all but 1 tablespoon fat from skillet; add onion to bacon fat in skillet and sauté until tender, about 3 minutes. Stir in egg yolks, salt, pepper, grated cheese and bacon.

4. Using electric mixer at high speed, beat egg whites in medium bowl until stiff; fold into onion-bacon mixture.

5. Mound mixture on top of toast squares; place on toaster oven tray. Set toaster oven at "broil"; broil hors d'oeuvres until lightly browned and puffy, about 5 minutes.

Makes 16 hors d'oeuvres.

cheese-wrapped olives

½ cup flour
¼ cup vegetable shortening
½ cup grated sharp Cheddar cheese
⅛ teaspoon cayenne pepper
1 tablespoon ice water
36 pimiento-stuffed olives

1. Place flour in medium bowl; using two knives or a pastry blender, cut shortening into flour until mixture resembles coarse cornmeal. Stir in grated cheese and cayenne pepper.

2. Sprinkle with ice water and knead to form a ball. (This is a very rich pastry requiring little water.)

3. Divide dough into quarters. Roll out each into 8 x 2-inch strip. Place 9 olives lengthwise down center of dough. Fold over edges of dough to form a roll. Wrap each roll in plastic wrap; chill for at least 3 hours.

4. Preheat toaster oven to 375° F for 2 minutes. Cut rolls into ¼-inch slices; place on toaster oven tray. Bake for 10 minutes or until golden.

Makes 6 dozen.

cheese straws

1 cup all-purpose flour
¼ cup butter or margarine
½ cup grated sharp Cheddar cheese
1 tablespoon sesame seeds
½ teaspoon salt
2 tablespoons cold water
1 teaspoon Worcestershire sauce

1. Place flour in medium bowl; using two knives or a pastry blender, cut butter or margarine into flour until mixture resembles coarse cornmeal. Stir in grated cheese, sesame seeds and salt.

2. Sprinkle with cold water and Worcestershire sauce and lightly knead to form a smooth ball. Roll out half of dough at a time to ¼-inch thickness on lightly floured board.

3. Cut into 4 x ¼-inch straws; twist each twice and place on toaster oven tray. Bake at 350° F for 10 to 12 minutes or until golden.

Makes about 3 dozen.

shrimp toast canapés

8 slices white bread
½ pound cooked, shelled, deveined shrimp, finely chopped
⅓ cup dry seasoned bread crumbs
2 tablespoons grated onion
1 tablespoon soy sauce
1 tablespoon cornstarch
¼ teaspoon salt
1 egg, slightly beaten

1. Trim crusts from bread. Lightly toast each slice in toaster oven; cut each into 4 squares and set aside.

2. In medium bowl, toss together finely chopped shrimp, bread crumbs, onion, soy sauce, cornstarch, salt and slightly beaten egg.

3. Spread mixture over toast squares; place on toaster oven tray. Set toaster oven at "broil"; broil canapés for 5 to 6 minutes, until they are lightly browned.

Makes 32 canapés.

sausage-stuffed mushrooms

1 pound medium-size fresh mushrooms
½ pound bulk sausage meat
⅓ cup grated Parmesan cheese
⅓ cup dry seasoned bread crumbs
½ teaspoon pepper
2 eggs, beaten
½ cup dry white wine or chicken broth

1. Wipe mushrooms thoroughly with damp paper towels. Remove stems; reserve for another use.

2. Brown sausage meat in medium skillet over medium heat, stirring constantly to break meat into small pieces; drain off surplus fat. Remove skillet from heat.

3. Add grated cheese, bread crumbs, pepper and beaten eggs to sausage meat in skillet; toss to blend well.

4. Fill mushroom caps with stuffing. Place on toaster oven tray; set in toaster oven. Pour wine or chicken broth over mushrooms. Bake at 350° F for 15 minutes or until mushrooms are tender.

Makes about 3 dozen.

meal for two

2 minute steaks, ½ inch thick
½ teaspoon salt
¼ teaspoon pepper
1 clove garlic, split
1 large tomato
2 canned pear halves
¼ cup butter or margarine
1 teaspoon snipped fresh or frozen chives
2 teaspoons horseradish, drained
one 3-ounce can potato sticks

1. Sprinkle both sides of steaks with salt and pepper. Rub all surfaces with split garlic clove. Place steaks on foil-lined toaster oven tray.

2. Cut tomato in half; place beside steaks. Place pear halves on tray.

3. Blend 2 tablespoons of the butter or margarine with the chives; place half of mixture on each tomato half. Blend remaining butter or margarine with drained horseradish; place half of mixture in each pear cavity.

4. Set toaster oven to "broil"; broil steaks and accompaniments for 5 minutes. Turn steaks; broil 5 minutes longer, adding potato sticks wrapped in foil to warm.

Serves 2.

meat loaf for four

1 pound ground beef
½ cup dry seasoned bread crumbs
¼ cup chopped golden raisins
¼ cup chopped parsley
1 clove garlic, crushed
1 envelope beef powder concentrate
1 teaspoon salt
¼ teaspoon pepper
1 egg, slightly beaten
¼ cup ketchup
¼ cup milk
½ cup apricot preserves

1. In large bowl, combine ground beef, bread crumbs, raisins, parsley, garlic, beef concentrate, salt and pepper.

2. In small bowl, beat together slightly beaten egg, ketchup and milk. Toss with meat mixture, mixing well. Shape into oval meat loaf; place on toaster oven tray. Bake at 350° F for 40 to 45 minutes.

3. Meanwhile, melt apricot preserves in small saucepan; brush over meat loaf several times during last 20 minutes of cooking time.

Serves 4.

barbecue-style chicken breasts

4 chicken breast halves, boned
½ cup vegetable oil
¼ cup red wine vinegar
¼ cup finely chopped onion
1 clove garlic, crushed
¼ teaspoon salt
⅛ teaspoon pepper
¾ cup prepared barbecue sauce

1. Wash chicken breasts under cold running water; pat dry with paper towels.

2. In shallow baking dish, combine oil, vinegar, onion, garlic, salt and pepper. Place chicken in marinade, turning to coat well. Cover and chill for at least 4 hours, turning occasionally.

3. Preheat toaster oven to 350° F for 2 minutes. Remove chicken from marinade with slotted spatula; place on toaster oven tray. Bake for 5 minutes. Spoon barbecue sauce over each chicken breast half; bake 15 minutes longer.

Serves 4.

macaroni and cheese

1 cup uncooked elbow macaroni
2 tablespoons butter or margarine
1 tablespoon flour
¾ cup milk
½ cup grated sharp Cheddar cheese
¼ teaspoon salt
3 to 4 drops hot pepper sauce
¼ cup dry seasoned bread crumbs

1. Cook macaroni according to label directions; drain.

2. Meanwhile, melt 1 tablespoon of the butter or margarine in small saucepan over low heat; stir in flour and cook for 2 minutes or until mixture bubbles.

3. Remove from heat; gradually add milk, stirring to keep mixture smooth. Return to heat; bring to boiling point, stirring constantly until mixture thickens.

4. Blend in grated cheese, salt and hot pepper sauce; stir until cheese is melted. Add drained macaroni to cheese sauce. Pour into lightly greased 9 x 5 x 3-inch loaf pan.

5. Melt remaining butter or margarine in small saucepan; stir in bread crumbs. Spread on top of macaroni. Bake in toaster oven at 375° F for 25 to 30 minutes.

Serves 4.

cheese and spinach strata

1 cup light cream

3 eggs

1 tablespoon Worcestershire sauce

½ teaspoon salt

one 10-ounce package frozen chopped spinach, thawed

½ cup chopped green onions

1 cup grated Swiss cheese

1. In small bowl, beat together cream, eggs, Worcestershire sauce and salt until well blended.

2. Drain thawed spinach in fine sieve, pressing out all water. Place half of spinach over bottom of lightly greased 9 x 5 x 3-inch loaf pan. Top with half of green onions and half of grated cheese. Repeat layers. Pour cream-egg mixture over top; let stand for 5 minutes.

3. Preheat toaster oven to 350° F for 2 minutes. Bake casserole for 35 to 45 minutes, until firm or until knife inserted in center comes out clean.

Serves 4.

stuffed onions

4 large onions

1 cup uncooked long-grain rice

½ pound ground beef

½ teaspoon salt

¼ teaspoon pepper

two 8-ounce cans tomato sauce

¼ cup water

¼ cup grated Parmesan cheese

1. Peel onions; place in large saucepan and cover with salted water. Bring to boiling point over medium heat; reduce heat and simmer until almost tender, about 15 minutes. Cook rice according to label directions.

2. Meanwhile, brown ground beef in medium skillet over low heat, stirring constantly to break meat into small pieces. Stir in salt, pepper, tomato sauce and water; simmer for 2 minutes. Stir in cooked rice.

3. Cool onions. Cut ½-inch slice from top of each; hollow out all but ½ inch of shell. Fill onion shells with rice mixture; sprinkle top of each with 1 tablespoon grated cheese. Place on toaster oven tray. Bake at 375° F for 25 to 30 minutes, until onions are very hot and tender.

Serves 4.

shrimp-stuffed tomatoes

4 medium tomatoes

2 tablespoons butter or margarine

½ cup chopped celery

½ cup chopped onion

two 4½-ounce cans tiny shrimp, drained

½ cup dry seasoned bread crumbs

½ teaspoon salt

¼ teaspoon pepper

1. Wash and dry tomatoes; cut ½-inch slice from top of each. Using a teaspoon, scoop out pulp and seeds; save for use in soups or sauces. Set tomato shells aside.

2. Melt butter or margarine in medium saucepan over medium heat; add celery and onion and sauté until tender, about 4 minutes. Add drained shrimp, bread crumbs, salt and pepper; stir to blend well. Stuff tomato shells with mixture.

3. Place stuffed tomatoes on toaster oven tray. Bake at 350° F for 20 to 25 minutes or until tomato shells are tender.

Serves 4.

zucchini bake

½ pound bulk sausage meat

½ cup chopped onion

1 clove garlic, crushed

1 teaspoon salt

¼ teaspoon pepper

one 15½-ounce jar spaghetti sauce

2 cups thinly sliced zucchini

1 cup grated mozzarella cheese

1. Brown sausage meat in medium skillet over medium heat, stirring constantly to break meat into small pieces. Remove from skillet with slotted spoon; set aside.

2. Pour all but 2 tablespoons drippings from skillet; add onion and garlic to drippings in skillet and sauté until onion is tender, about 4 minutes. Stir in salt, pepper, spaghetti sauce and sausage meat.

3. In lightly greased 9 x 5 x 3-inch loaf pan, layer 1 cup of the zucchini slices, half of sausage-tomato mixture and ½ cup of the grated cheese. Repeat layers using remaining ingredients.

4. Bake in toaster oven at 350° F for 35 to 40 minutes. Let stand for 5 minutes before serving.

Serves 4.

beef and cheese heroes

eight ¼-inch-thick onion slices

¼ cup butter or margarine, melted

eight ¼-inch-thick tomato slices

2 individual hero sandwich rolls, each 6 inches long

2 tablespoons prepared mustard

½ pound sliced cooked roast beef

4 slices Swiss cheese

1. Preheat toaster oven to "broil"; place onion slices on foil-lined toaster oven tray. Brush with a little of the melted butter or margarine; broil for 5 minutes. Add tomato slices to tray; brush with a little of the melted butter or margarine. Broil 2 minutes longer.

2. Cut sandwich rolls in half; brush cut surfaces with remaining melted butter or margarine and spread with mustard. Layer half of roast beef on bottom half of each roll; top each with 4 onion slices and 4 tomato slices, arranged alternately in overlapping line. Fold cheese slices in half; arrange 2 slices on top of each sandwich.

3. Place tops of rolls cut side up in toaster oven beside prepared sandwiches. Set toaster oven to "broil"; broil until cheese melts and rolls are toasted. Place tops over cheese.

Serves 2.

open-face chicken sandwiches

2 slices whole wheat bread

3 tablespoons Dijon-style mustard

½ pound sliced precooked chicken roll

1 tablespoon butter or margarine

1 tablespoon flour

⅔ cup milk

½ teaspoon grated lemon rind

⅛ teaspoon pepper

paprika

1. Lightly toast whole wheat bread in toaster oven; spread one side of each slice with a little of the mustard.

2. Spread one side of each chicken slice with remaining mustard; fold each slice in half. Arrange chicken slices in overlapping line to cover each toast slice. Place on toaster oven tray.

3. Melt butter or margarine in small saucepan over low heat; stir in flour and cook until mixture bubbles, about 2 to 3 minutes, stirring constantly.

4. Remove from heat; gradually add milk, stirring to keep mixture smooth. Return to heat; bring to boiling point, stirring constantly until mixture thickens. Stir in lemon rind and pepper.

5. Spoon cream sauce over chicken; sprinkle lightly with paprika. Bake in toaster oven at 325° F for 15 minutes.

Serves 2.

grilled ham and cheese sandwiches

2 sesame seed hamburger buns

2 tablespoons butter or margarine

1 tablespoon horseradish, drained

1 large tomato, thinly sliced

½ pound precooked ham slices

4 slices Swiss cheese

1 tablespoon prepared spicy mustard

1. Split hamburger buns in half. Blend butter or margarine with horseradish; spread over cut sides of buns. Lightly toast bottom halves in toaster oven.

2. Place tomato slices over toasted buns; top with ham slices. Spread cheese slices lightly with mustard; fold in half and place on top of ham slices.

3. Place both bottoms and tops of hamburger buns on toaster oven tray. Set toaster oven at "broil"; heat until cheese melts and tops of buns are lightly toasted. Place tops of buns over cheese.

Serves 4.

new york reuben sandwiches

4 slices pumpernickel bread

1 tablespoon butter or margarine

½ pound sliced corned beef or pastrami

one 8-ounce can sauerkraut, rinsed and drained

2 slices Swiss cheese

¼ cup Russian salad dressing

1. Spread one side of each bread slice with a little butter or margarine. For each sandwich, layer half of corned beef or pastrami, half of rinsed, drained sauerkraut, 1 slice cheese (trimming to fit) and 2 tablespoons Russian dressing on buttered side of 1 bread slice. Top with second bread slice, buttered side down.

2. Wrap each sandwich in foil. Place on toaster oven tray. Bake at 350° F for 15 minutes, until sandwich is hot and cheese is melted.

Serves 2. Shown on page 67.

EnergySaving Tip: Foods like sandwiches and potatoes wrapped in aluminum foil will stay warm in or out of the oven long after the heat has been switched off. Foil-wrapped foods can also finish cooking in residual oven heat—switch the oven off 5 minutes before the end of the cooking time specified in the recipe, and leave the sandwiches or other foil-wrapped food in the oven for 5 additional minutes. These extra minutes in the oven will add up to a lot of savings in your energy budget.

hot crab snack sandwiches

2 English muffins

one 6-ounce package frozen crabmeat, thawed and drained

⅓ cup finely chopped celery

¼ cup sour cream

1 tablespoon finely chopped onion

½ teaspoon Worcestershire sauce

¼ teaspoon salt

4 thin slices sharp Cheddar cheese

1. Split English muffins in half; toast lightly in toaster oven. Set aside.

2. In medium bowl, flake crabmeat with fork. Blend in celery, sour cream, onion, Worcestershire sauce and salt.

3. Spoon crab mixture on top of each muffin half; top each with cheese slice. Place on toaster oven tray. Set toaster oven at "broil"; broil for 5 minutes, until crabmeat is hot and cheese is melted.

Serves 4.

sesame seed cheese biscuits

2 cups packaged biscuit mix

1 cup grated sharp Cheddar cheese

¼ cup grated onion

3 tablespoons sesame seeds

¾ cup milk

2 to 3 drops hot pepper sauce

1. Preheat toaster oven to 400° F.

2. In large bowl, combine biscuit mix, grated cheese, grated onion and 2 tablespoons of the sesame seeds. Combine milk and hot pepper sauce; add all at once to dry ingredients. Stir lightly with fork to form soft dough.

3. Turn dough out onto lightly floured board. Knead gently 3 or 4 times to form smooth ball. Roll or pat into ½-inch-thick circle. Cut into 2-inch rounds; place on ungreased toaster oven tray.

4. Bake for 15 to 20 minutes or until biscuits are brown and puffed; 5 minutes before end of cooking time, brush with a little milk and sprinkle with remaining sesame seeds.

Makes 10.

upside-down coffee cake

2 cups packaged biscuit mix

one 8-ounce can crushed
  pineapple, drained

½ cup sugar

¼ cup finely chopped walnuts

1 egg

¼ cup milk

1 teaspoon almond extract

STREUSEL

½ cup brown sugar, firmly
  packed

½ cup finely chopped walnuts

¼ cup flour

2 tablespoons butter or
  margarine, melted

1. Preheat toaster oven to 350° F.

2. In large bowl, blend together biscuit mix, drained pineapple, sugar and ¼ cup chopped walnuts. In small bowl, beat together egg, milk and almond extract. Pour over dry ingredients; beat to blend well. Pour into well-greased 9 x 5 x 3-inch loaf pan.

3. To make streusel, combine brown sugar, ½ cup chopped walnuts and flour in small bowl; stir in melted butter or margarine with fork. Sprinkle mixture over cake batter.

4. Bake for 40 to 45 minutes or until cake is brown and firm to the touch. (Streusel mixture will sink to bottom of pan during baking.) Cool on wire rack for 5 minutes, loosening sides of cake with spatula. Unmold on wire rack; cool 30 minutes longer. Serve warm.

Makes 1 coffee cake.

almond pinwheel swirls

one 8-ounce can almond paste

one 8-ounce package
  refrigerator crescent rolls

⅓ cup butter or margarine,
  melted

⅓ cup sugar

¾ teaspoon cinnamon

¼ cup red currant jelly, melted

1. Roll out almond paste between two sheets of waxed paper to form 13 x 7-inch rectangle; set aside.

2. Unroll 2 crescent roll dough sections on lightly floured board; press dough lightly to join 2 halves and seal perforations.

3. Lightly brush dough with half of the melted butter or margarine; sprinkle with half of mixture of sugar and cinnamon. Top with almond paste; brush top of almond paste with melted currant jelly.

4. Roll up jelly-roll fashion, working from one long edge. Cut crosswise into 24 slices, each ½ inch thick. Brush cut sides with remaining melted butter or margarine and sprinkle with remaining cinnamon sugar.

5. Preheat toaster oven to 375° F for 2 minutes. Place 8 swirls at a time on toaster oven tray and bake for 10 to 12 minutes or until golden. Chill remaining swirls until time to bake.

Makes 24.

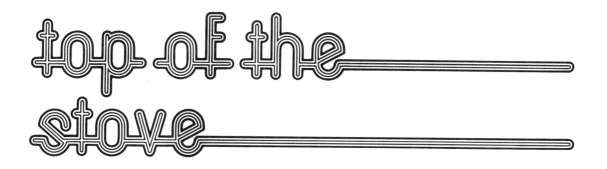

top of the stove

Whether you boiled your first pot of water at age nine or delayed the inevitable kitchen confrontation until you moved into your own apartment, you're probably most familiar with top-of-the-stove cooking. It's available at the turn of a dial, easily controlled and monitored, and requires no wasteful preheating. And your mother probably advised you to make big pots of soup, stew and sauce to have some left over for another day. So what's new about top-of-the-stove cooking? Plenty!

Top-of-the-stove convenience foods—whether they're frozen, canned or freeze-dried—are quick and easy to prepare. Not only are these products work and time savers, they let us enjoy the fruits of summer in the dead of winter. And it's easy enough to add sparkle and dash to these prepared foods with judicious seasoning and clever accompaniments of other fresh foods. But don't overheat any of these convenience foods, or you'll cancel their value as energy savers.

What else is new? The pressure cooker is making a comeback! This handy gadget is a godsend for working cooks. Because it can handle large quantities of food in one-third of the usual cooking time, it's ideal for recipes that normally require extensive simmering. A busy cook can turn out spicy Lamb and Onion Curry or Speedy Stuffed Peppers in less than an hour. A pressure cooker can be a wonderful addition to your kitchen, but be sure to follow the manufacturer's operating directions for optimum safety when you use it.

Bubble, bubble, boil and sizzle; fry it; simmer it; stew it. If you still think there's nothing new to top-of-the-stove cooking, try some of these tantalizers—Chinese Steak Salad, Savory Skillet Chicken with Noodles, Hot Bean and Onion Salad—and tickle your taste buds.

pan steak italian

1½ pounds round steak

1 teaspoon instant meat tenderizer

¼ cup flour

1 teaspoon salt

¼ teaspoon pepper

¼ cup butter or margarine

one 16-ounce can crushed tomatoes

⅓ cup chopped onion

⅓ cup chopped green pepper

1 clove garlic, crushed

½ teaspoon oregano

1 cup grated mozzarella cheese

1. Sprinkle both sides of round steak with meat tenderizer; pierce both sides of steak with long-tined fork according to tenderizer label instructions.

2. Mix flour, salt and pepper. Cut steak into 4 equal portions and coat with flour mixture.

3. Melt butter or margarine in large broiler-proof skillet over medium heat; add meat and sauté until golden brown, about 2 to 3 minutes per side. Add tomatoes, onion, green pepper, garlic and oregano. Reduce heat to low and simmer, covered, until meat is tender, about 20 to 30 minutes, depending on thickness of steak.

4. Preheat broiler.

5. Sprinkle grated cheese over meat; broil 3 inches from heat to melt cheese. (Or cover and simmer 2 to 3 minutes longer to melt cheese.)

Serves 4.

savory boiled beef

5-pound beef brisket, cut into ¾-inch cubes

two 16-ounce cans or packages sauerkraut

one 24-ounce can vegetable-tomato juice

4 large onions, peeled and quartered

12 peppercorns

½ cup brown sugar, firmly packed

2 teaspoons Worcestershire sauce

1. In 8-quart Dutch oven, combine beef cubes, undrained sauerkraut, vegetable-tomato juice, onions, peppercorns, brown sugar and Worcestershire sauce.

2. Bring mixture to boiling point over medium heat, stirring constantly. Reduce heat to low and simmer, covered, for 1 hour or until meat is tender. Serve half of Savory Boiled Beef immediately, placing in heatproof casserole.

DOUBLE BATCH

3. Cool remaining beef; place in freezer container and seal tightly. Freeze up to 3 months.

4. To serve, thaw, covered, in refrigerator overnight. Place in heatproof 4-quart casserole and simmer for 10 to 15 minutes.

Each half serves 4 to 6.

chinese steak salad

2 pounds round steak

2 tablespoons Worcestershire sauce

2 teaspoons salt

¼ cup vegetable oil

2 cups julienne strips sweet red pepper

1 cup thinly sliced onion rings

2 cloves garlic, crushed

2 teaspoons oregano

¼ cup red wine vinegar

1. Wipe steak well with damp paper towels; cut across grain to slice meat into 2 x ¼-inch strips. Toss meat with Worcestershire sauce and 1 teaspoon of the salt in large bowl; let stand for 15 minutes.

2. Heat 2 tablespoons of the oil in large skillet over medium heat; add red pepper, onion rings, garlic and oregano and sauté until pepper and onion are crisp-tender. Sprinkle in remaining 1 teaspoon salt and stir constantly for about 3 minutes. Remove vegetables from skillet with slotted spoon; set aside.

3. Add remaining 2 tablespoons oil to skillet; remove beef strips from marinade, add to skillet and sauté until just cooked, about 3 to 4 minutes, stirring constantly.

4. Return vegetables to skillet; add vinegar. Heat for 1 minute, stirring constantly. Serve half of steak as entrée with hot white rice.

To serve cold: Cool and chill remaining Chinese steak. Serve as salad on bed of lettuce leaves with tomato slices.

Each half serves 4. Both hot and cold versions shown on page 65.

brisket pot roast stew

5-pound beef brisket, cut into 1-inch cubes

½ cup flour

½ teaspoon pepper

½ cup butter or margarine

1½ cups chopped onions

2 cloves garlic, crushed

1 cup dry red wine

1 cup beef broth

1 cup sour cream

chopped parsley

1. Toss beef cubes in mixture of flour and pepper to coat. Melt butter or margarine in 8-quart Dutch oven over medium heat; add beef cubes a few at a time and sauté until brown. Remove meat as browned and set aside.

2. Add onions and garlic to drippings in pan; sauté until onions are tender, about 5 minutes, stirring constantly. Return browned meat to Dutch oven.

3. Add wine and beef broth to pan. Reduce heat to low and simmer, covered, until meat is tender, about 1½ hours. Stir in sour cream; heat for 2 minutes but do not boil. Serve half of Brisket Pot Roast Stew immediately, placing in casserole and garnishing with parsley.

DOUBLE BATCH

4. Cool remaining stew; place in freezer container and seal tightly. Freeze up to 3 months.

5. To serve, thaw, covered, in refrigerator overnight. Place in heat-proof 4-quart casserole and simmer for 10 to 15 minutes. Garnish with chopped parsley.

Each half serves 4 to 6.

beef brisket

3½- to 4-pound beef brisket
2 tablespoons butter or margarine
1 cup chopped onion
1 clove garlic, crushed
2 envelopes beef powder concentrate
3 cups water
2 tablespoons flour
1 tablespoon horseradish, drained
¼ teaspoon pepper

1. Wipe beef brisket well with damp paper towels; trim off and discard any surplus fat from top surface. Melt butter or margarine in 4-quart Dutch oven or large heavy saucepan over medium-low heat; add beef brisket and sauté for about 10 minutes, turning to brown all sides. Remove from pan and set aside.

2. Add onion and garlic to drippings in Dutch oven; sauté until tender, about 4 minutes, stirring constantly. Stir in beef concentrate and water; bring to boiling point. Return brisket to pan.

3. Reduce heat to low and simmer, covered, for 2½ to 3 hours or until beef is tender. Remove beef brisket to heated serving platter; keep warm.

4. In small bowl, blend flour with a little water; stir into pan liquid. Bring to boiling point over medium heat, stirring constantly; reduce heat to low and simmer for 5 minutes. Stir in drained horseradish and pepper.

5. Serve half of Beef Brisket, slicing across grain of meat; accompany with pan gravy.

To serve cold: Cool and chill remaining Beef Brisket. Use as a sandwich filling or as part of a salad, accompanied by horseradish or spicy mustard if desired.

Each half serves 4.

chili con carne

¼ cup vegetable oil
1½ pounds ground chuck beef
1 cup chopped onion
2 cloves garlic, crushed
4 cups tomato juice
1½ teaspoons salt
1½ teaspoons chili powder
1 teaspoon paprika
½ teaspoon red pepper flakes
two 15½-ounce cans red kidney
    beans, drained
½ cup chopped parsley

1. Heat oil in large skillet or saucepan over medium heat; add ground beef, onion and garlic and sauté for 10 minutes, stirring constantly to break meat into small pieces.

2. Add tomato juice, salt, chili powder, paprika and red pepper. Bring to boiling point, stirring constantly; reduce heat to low and simmer, covered, for 10 minutes.

3. Add drained kidney beans; cover and simmer 10 minutes longer. Sprinkle with parsley just before serving.

Serves 4.

summer-winter beef and vegetables

4- to 5-pound corned beef
    brisket
2 tablespoons butter or
    margarine
1 clove garlic, crushed
12 peppercorns
8 medium potatoes
8 medium carrots

    SAUCE

1 cup sour cream
2 tablespoons milk
2 tablespoons snipped fresh
    dill, or 2 teaspoons dried dill
1 teaspoon salt

1. Wipe corned beef brisket well with damp paper towels. Melt butter or margarine in 8-quart Dutch oven over medium heat; add brisket and sauté for about 5 minutes, turning quickly to brown all sides.

2. Add cold water to cover; add garlic and peppercorns. Bring to boiling point. Reduce heat to low and simmer, covered, for 3¼ to 4 hours or until meat is tender.

3. Peel and halve potatoes; peel carrots and cut into 2-inch pieces. Add potatoes and carrots to Dutch oven 30 minutes before end of cooking time.

4. Meanwhile, make sauce by blending sour cream, milk, dill and salt in medium bowl. Chill until serving time. Remove meat and vegetables from cooking liquid. Slice meat thinly across grain; serve half of meat hot accompanied by half of vegetables; spoon half of sauce over the vegetables.

To serve cold: Cool and chill remaining meat. Toss remaining vegetables in remaining sauce and chill. Serve as a cold meat-and-vegetable salad platter.

Each half serves 4.

quick new england boiled dinner

2 cups double-strength beef broth

8 silverskin onions, peeled

6 new or small potatoes

6 whole carrots, peeled

4 to 6 parsnips, peeled

1 small head cabbage, cut into 4 wedges

1½ pounds sliced pastrami

1. Bring double-strength beef broth to boiling point in 6- to 8-quart Dutch oven. Add onions, potatoes, carrots and parsnips; simmer, covered, over low heat for 20 minutes.

2. Add cabbage wedges; simmer, covered, for 10 minutes. Place sliced pastrami on top of vegetables; cook 5 minutes longer. Serve meat and vegetables with prepared mustard and horseradish.

Serves 4.

Note: Make double-strength broth by using double the amount of powder or cubes called for in label directions.

top-of-stove shepherd's pie

2 tablespoons butter or margarine

1 cup chopped onion

1 tablespoon flour

1 envelope beef powder concentrate

¾ cup dry red wine or water

one 12-ounce can corned beef

one 8-ounce can whole kernel corn, drained

1⅓ cups instant mashed potatoes

½ cup grated sharp Cheddar cheese

1. Melt butter or margarine in large skillet over medium heat; add onion and sauté until tender, about 4 minutes, stirring constantly.

2. Sprinkle flour and beef concentrate over onion; stir in wine or water. Bring to boiling point, stirring constantly. Reduce heat to low. Crumble corned beef with fork; add to skillet along with drained corn. Heat, covered, for 5 minutes.

3. Meanwhile, prepare instant mashed potatoes according to label directions to yield 4 servings. Beat cheese into hot potatoes.

4. Spoon corned beef mixture into 8 x 8 x 2-inch baking dish. Swirl hot potatoes over corned beef; serve immediately.

Serves 4.

home-style veal stew

¼ cup butter or margarine

1½ pounds veal shoulder, cut into ¾-inch cubes

½ cup chopped onion

1 clove garlic, crushed

one 8-ounce can tomato sauce

¼ cup chopped parsley

1 tablespoon soy sauce

4 cups beef broth or consommé

2 cups cubed potatoes

one 10-ounce package frozen peas and carrots

1. Melt butter or margarine in 4- to 6-quart Dutch oven over medium heat; add veal cubes a few at a time and sauté, turning to brown all sides. Remove meat as browned and set aside.

2. Add onion and garlic to drippings in pan; sauté until onion is tender, about 5 minutes, stirring constantly.

3. Return veal to Dutch oven; blend in tomato sauce, parsley and soy sauce. Add beef broth or consommé; bring to boiling point. Reduce heat to low and simmer, covered, for 30 minutes or until veal is tender.

4. Add potatoes and simmer for 10 minutes. Add frozen peas and carrots; simmer 5 minutes longer or until vegetables are tender.

Serves 4.

quick curried lamb

¼ cup butter or margarine

¼ cup chopped onion

¼ cup flour

1 to 2 tablespoons curry powder

½ teaspoon ginger

½ teaspoon salt

2 cups chicken broth

1 cup half-and-half or light cream

3 cups cubed cooked lamb, or 1-pound precooked ham slice, cubed

1 apple, peeled, cored and chopped

¼ cup chutney

2 tablespoons lemon juice

1. Melt butter or margarine in large saucepan over medium heat; add onion and sauté until tender, about 5 minutes, stirring constantly. Stir in flour, curry, ginger and salt; stir and cook 2 minutes longer.

2. Stir in chicken broth. Add half-and-half or cream and bring to boiling point, stirring constantly.

3. Reduce heat to low; stir in lamb or ham. Cover and simmer until meat is hot, about 5 minutes.

4. Add apple, chutney and lemon juice; stir to blend. Heat until apple is semi-cooked; do not let mixture boil.

Serves 4.

pork and herbed dumplings

2 tablespoons butter or margarine

1 cup onion rings

1 cup sliced apple

one 16-ounce can or package sauerkraut

2 teaspoons caraway seeds

1 cup water

1½ pounds precooked pork roll, cut into ¾-inch cubes

DUMPLINGS

¾ cup water

¼ cup butter or margarine

1½ cups packaged herb stuffing mix

2 eggs, slightly beaten

½ teaspoon celery salt

1. Melt 2 tablespoons butter or margarine in 4- to 6-quart Dutch oven over medium heat; add onion and apple and sauté until golden brown, about 3 to 4 minutes, stirring constantly.

2. Add undrained sauerkraut, caraway seeds and 1 cup water. Stir to mix well; add pork and stir again. Reduce heat to low and simmer, covered, for 20 minutes.

3. Meanwhile, make dumplings by heating ¾ cup water and ¼ cup butter or margarine in medium saucepan over medium heat until butter is melted; stir in packaged stuffing mix, slightly beaten eggs and celery salt.

4. Form stuffing mixture into walnut-size balls; drop onto pork and sauerkraut. Cover tightly and steam for 15 minutes.

Serves 4.

stove-top sausage

1 pound bulk sausage meat

1 cup chopped onion

½ cup chopped green pepper

one 20-ounce can whole tomatoes

one 8-ounce package egg noodles

½ cup grated sharp Cheddar cheese

1. Brown sausage meat in large skillet over medium heat, stirring constantly to break meat into small pieces. Remove meat from skillet with slotted spoon; set aside.

2. Pour all but 2 tablespoons fat from skillet; add onion and green pepper to skillet and sauté until onion is golden, about 5 minutes.

3. Add tomatoes to skillet, stirring to mix well and breaking into small pieces with back of spoon. Add sausage meat; reduce heat to low and simmer, covered, until meat and vegetables are tender, about 20 to 25 minutes.

4. Meanwhile, cook egg noodles according to label directions. Drain well; toss with meat-tomato mixture in skillet. Add grated cheese; heat until noodles are piping hot and cheese is melted.

Serves 4.

lunchtime franks and macaroni

one 7½-ounce package
    macaroni and cheese dinner

½ pound frankfurters, cut into
    ½-inch slices

½ cup finely chopped onion

¾ teaspoon salt

¼ teaspoon pepper

⅓ cup milk

¼ cup chopped parsley

1. Mix macaroni and cheese dinner according to label directions in medium saucepan or 1½-quart heatproof casserole. Stir in frankfurters, onion, salt, pepper and milk.

2. Cook, covered, over low heat for 15 to 20 minutes or until macaroni is tender. Sprinkle with parsley; serve immediately.

Serves 4.

mother hubbard sandwiches

8 slices whole wheat bread

¼ cup butter or margarine,
    softened

one 5-ounce jar sharp
    processed cheese spread,
    softened

one 7-ounce can chunk-style
    ham

¼ cup chopped dill pickle

¼ cup mayonnaise

1. Assemble sandwiches on cookie sheet. Spread one side of each bread slice with some softened butter or margarine. Place buttered side down on cookie sheet. Spread second side of each bread slice with some softened cheese spread.

2. In small bowl, blend chunk-style ham, chopped pickle and mayonnaise. Spread ham mixture over 4 bread slices; top with remaining slices, buttered side up. Fry sandwiches on hot griddle or in large skillet until bread is browned and filling is hot, 2 minutes per side.

Serves 4.

skillet chicken orange

2½- to 3-pound broiler-fryer
    chicken, cut into serving pieces

¼ cup butter or margarine

3 tablespoons flour

¼ cup currant jelly

½ teaspoon salt

¼ teaspoon ginger

¼ teaspoon nutmeg

1½ cups orange juice

2 medium oranges, peeled
    and sectioned

1. Wash chicken under cold running water; pat dry with paper towels. Melt butter or margarine in large skillet over medium heat; add chicken pieces a few at a time and sauté until golden brown on all sides, about 5 to 8 minutes. Remove chicken as browned and set aside.

2. Blend flour and currant jelly into drippings in skillet; cook over low heat, stirring to make very smooth. Blend in salt, ginger and nutmeg. Slowly add orange juice, stirring to keep mixture smooth. Bring to boiling point over medium heat, stirring constantly.

3. Return chicken pieces to skillet, turning in sauce to coat well. Reduce heat to low and simmer, covered, until chicken is well cooked, 30 to 40 minutes. Add oranges 5 minutes before end of cooking time.

Serves 4. Shown on page 68.

chicken stew

two 3-pound broiler-fryer chickens, quartered

2 cups water

¼ cup molasses

4 small yellow onions, peeled and halved

4 whole cloves

2 teaspoons salt

1 bay leaf

2 cups sliced celery, in ½-inch slices

2 cups sliced carrots, in ½-inch slices

2 cups milk

½ cup flour

chopped celery leaves

1. Wash chicken pieces under cold running water; place in 8-quart Dutch oven. Add water, molasses, onions, cloves, salt and bay leaf. Simmer, covered, over low heat for 1 to 1½ hours or until chicken pieces are tender.

2. Remove cloves and bay leaf. Add celery and carrots; continue to simmer over low heat until vegetables are tender, about 20 minutes.

3. Remove meat and vegetables from broth; set aside. Measure and reserve 2 cups broth; cool and freeze any extra broth for later use.

4. In Dutch oven, slowly blend a little of the milk with the flour until smooth. Add remaining milk and reserved chicken broth; bring to boiling point over low heat, stirring constantly until mixture thickens. Stir in chicken and vegetables; heat for 5 minutes. Serve half of stew immediately, placing in heatproof casserole and garnishing with chopped celery leaves.

DOUBLE BATCH

5. Cool remaining stew; place in freezer container and seal tightly. Freeze up to 2 months.

6. To serve, unseal and thaw in refrigerator overnight. Place stew in Dutch oven or large saucepan and reheat, covered, over low heat for 20 to 30 minutes, until very hot and bubbly.

Each half serves 4 to 6.

chicken and biscuits

one 10¾-ounce can cream of mushroom soup

¾ cup light cream or half-and-half

¼ cup dry sherry

two 6¾-ounce cans chunk-style chicken

one 8-ounce can water chestnuts, drained and sliced

one 11-ounce package heat-and-serve biscuits

1. In medium saucepan, combine mushroom soup, cream or half-and-half and sherry. Stir in chunk-style chicken and water chestnuts. Simmer, covered, over low heat until very hot, about 10 minutes.

2. Meanwhile, warm biscuits according to label directions. Split biscuits and place 2 halves on each of 4 serving plates; top with chicken mixture. Serve remaining biscuits alongside.

Serves 4.

chicken breasts chablis

4 chicken breast halves
½ teaspoon salt
¼ teaspoon pepper
¼ cup butter or margarine
1 cup Chablis or other dry white wine
½ cup currant jelly
½ cup grated Swiss cheese
¼ cup slivered almonds
1½ teaspoons mild paprika

1. Wash chicken breast halves under cold running water; pat dry with paper towels. Sprinkle chicken with salt and pepper.

2. Melt butter or margarine in large broiler-proof skillet over medium heat; add chicken breast halves and sauté until golden, about 4 minutes per side. Remove from skillet and set aside.

3. Blend wine and currant jelly into drippings in skillet; simmer over low heat until jelly is melted, stirring to keep mixture smooth.

4. Return chicken to skillet, turning in sauce to coat well. Simmer, covered, until chicken is well cooked, about 20 to 30 minutes.

5. Preheat broiler.

6. In small bowl, mix grated cheese, almonds and paprika; sprinkle over chicken. Broil 3 inches from heat to melt cheese and brown almonds, about 3 minutes. (Or cover and simmer 5 minutes longer to melt cheese.)

Serves 4.

chicken pot pie

one 9-inch frozen prepared pie shell
1 tablespoon flour
¾ cup light cream
2 cups diced cooked chicken
one 10-ounce package frozen creamed peas and pearl onions
1 teaspoon salt
1 teaspoon grated lemon rind
¼ teaspoon pepper
¼ cup chopped parsley
1 tablespoon paprika

1. Bake pie shell according to label directions. Meanwhile, make filling by blending flour and cream in medium saucepan until smooth. Bring to boiling point over medium heat, stirring constantly.

2. Stir in chicken, frozen peas and onions, salt, lemon rind and pepper. Reduce heat to low and simmer, covered, for 5 minutes, until chicken is hot and vegetables are tender.

3. Pour filling into baked pie shell. Sprinkle with parsley and paprika.

Serves 4.

chicken à la king

⅓ cup butter or margarine

½ cup chopped green pepper

one 8-ounce can sliced
  mushrooms

½ cup flour

1 teaspoon salt

2 cups chicken broth

2 cups milk

4 cups cubed cooked chicken,
  or 1½ pounds precooked
  chicken roll, cubed

¼ cup diced pimiento

1. Melt butter or margarine in large skillet over low heat; add green pepper and sauté until tender, about 3 minutes. Drain mushrooms, reserving liquid; add mushrooms to skillet.

2. Blend in flour and salt; cook, stirring constantly, until mixture bubbles. Remove from heat; slowly blend in reserved mushroom liquid, chicken broth and milk.

3. Return to heat; bring to boiling point, stirring constantly until mixture thickens. Add chicken and pimiento; heat 5 minutes longer. Serve half of Chicken à la King immediately over toast points.

DOUBLE BATCH

4. Cool remaining Chicken à la King as quickly as possible; place in freezer container and seal tightly. Freeze up to 2 months.

5. To serve, remove from container and place mixture in top of double boiler; set over simmering water. Reheat, covered, for 45 minutes. Serve over toast points.

Each half serves 4.

savory skillet chicken with noodles

2 tablespoons butter or
  margarine

½ cup chopped green pepper

¼ cup chopped onion

¼ cup chopped celery

¾ teaspoon salt

¼ teaspoon pepper

two 10½-ounce cans chicken à
  la king

2 tablespoons lemon juice

one 8-ounce package thin egg
  noodles

¼ cup chopped parsley

1. Melt butter or margarine in large skillet over medium heat; add green pepper, onion, celery, salt and pepper and sauté until vegetables are tender, about 5 to 7 minutes, stirring constantly.

2. Reduce heat to low; stir in chicken à la king and lemon juice. Simmer, covered, for 3 to 4 minutes or until mixture is very hot, stirring occasionally.

3. Meanwhile, cook noodles according to label directions; drain and toss with parsley. Serve chicken over hot noodles.

Serves 4.

double-rich creamed turkey

1½ cups chicken broth

¼ cup flour

½ cup mayonnaise

2 cups diced cooked turkey or turkey roll

one 10-ounce package frozen peas

one 3-ounce can sliced mushrooms, drained

¼ cup finely diced pimientos or roasted pepper

¼ cup grated sharp Cheddar cheese

4 English muffins, split and toasted

1. In medium bowl, slowly blend ½ cup of the chicken broth into flour; mix until smooth. Place mixture in large skillet or saucepan; add remaining broth. Bring to boiling point over medium heat, stirring constantly. Reduce heat to low; rapidly blend in mayonnaise, stirring to keep mixture smooth.

2. Add turkey, frozen peas, drained mushrooms and pimientos or pepper. Simmer, covered, until turkey is heated through and peas are tender, about 10 minutes.

3. Blend in grated cheese, stirring until cheese is melted. Serve creamed turkey over toasted English muffins, allowing 2 muffin halves per person.

Serves 4.

seafood risotto

¼ cup olive or vegetable oil

½ cup chopped onion

¼ cup chopped green pepper

1 clove garlic, crushed

1 cup uncooked long-grain rice

1½ cups vegetable bouillon

one 6-ounce can tomato paste

1 teaspoon crushed basil

1 pound fresh or frozen fish fillets (cod, haddock or other white fish), cut into 1-inch squares

one 10-ounce package frozen peas

one 3-ounce can mushrooms

1. Heat oil in large saucepan over medium heat; add onion, green pepper and garlic and sauté until onion and pepper are tender, about 5 minutes, stirring constantly. Stir in rice and sauté until lightly browned, about 5 minutes, stirring constantly.

2. Blend in vegetable bouillon, tomato paste and basil; bring to boiling point. Reduce heat to low and simmer, covered, for 25 to 30 minutes or until rice is barely tender.

3. Add fish squares, peas and undrained mushrooms. Blend gently into rice. Cover and simmer for 10 minutes longer or until fish flakes easily when tested with fork.

Serves 4.

spaghetti with tomato-clam sauce

two 10½-ounce cans tomato-
  clam sauce
1 teaspoon salt
1 teaspoon sugar
¼ teaspoon pepper
2 to 3 drops hot pepper sauce
one 16-ounce package
  spaghetti
½ cup grated Parmesan cheese

1. In medium saucepan, combine tomato-clam sauce, salt, sugar, pepper and hot pepper sauce. Simmer, covered, over low heat for 10 minutes.

2. Meanwhile, cook spaghetti according to label directions. Drain; toss with cheese. Divide among 4 individual serving bowls; top with tomato-clam sauce.

Serves 4.

japanese vegetables and shrimp

one 16-ounce polybag frozen
  Japanese-style vegetables
1 envelope chicken powder
  concentrate
1 teaspoon soy sauce
one 8-ounce can bean sprouts,
  drained
one 8-ounce package frozen
  tiny shrimp
1⅓ cups quick-cooking rice

1. Cook Japanese-style vegetables according to label directions in large skillet, adding chicken concentrate and soy sauce.

2. Stir in drained bean sprouts and frozen shrimp. Reduce heat to low and cook, covered, for 4 to 5 minutes or until shrimp is tender.

3. Cook rice according to label directions. Serve vegetable-shrimp mixture over hot rice.

Serves 4.

sherried tuna with rice

1 tablespoon butter or
  margarine
one 13-ounce can tuna, drained
one 15½-ounce can peas,
  drained
one 10¾-ounce can cream of
  chicken soup
¼ cup milk
¼ cup dry sherry
⅛ teaspoon pepper
⅛ teaspoon ginger
1⅓ cups quick-cooking rice

1. Melt butter or margarine in large skillet over medium heat; add drained tuna, stirring to break into small pieces. Stir in drained peas, cream of chicken soup, milk, sherry, pepper and ginger. Reduce heat to low and simmer, covered, for 10 minutes or until very hot, stirring occasionally.

2. Meanwhile, prepare rice according to label directions. Serve sherried tuna mixture over hot rice.

Serves 4.

green beans, hot or cold

2½ pounds fresh green beans,
    or one 32-ounce polybag
    frozen cut green beans
⅔ cup olive or vegetable oil
⅓ cup lemon juice
1 clove garlic, crushed
¼ teaspoon pepper
½ cup finely diced mozzarella
   cheese

1. Remove and discard ends from fresh green beans. Cut beans into 1-inch pieces and wash well. Place in large saucepan with salted water to cover; simmer over medium heat until crisp-tender, about 5 to 7 minutes. Or cook frozen beans according to label directions. Drain beans very well.

2. Add oil, lemon juice, garlic and pepper to beans in pan. Stir to blend well. Heat over low heat. Serve half of beans hot, sprinkled with ¼ cup of the diced cheese.

To serve cold: Cool remaining beans; add remaining ¼ cup diced cheese. Chill and serve as vegetable salad.

Each half serves 4.

hot bean and onion salad

½ cup olive oil
¼ cup red wine vinegar
1 clove garlic, crushed
1½ teaspoons salt
1 teaspoon oregano
¼ teaspoon pepper
one 15½-ounce can cut green
   beans, drained
one 15½-ounce can wax
   beans, drained
one 15½-ounce can red kidney
   beans, drained
1 cup thinly sliced onion rings
1 cup julienne strips green
   pepper

1. In medium saucepan, combine oil, vinegar, garlic, salt, oregano and pepper. Heat over low heat for 2 minutes.

2. Stir in drained green beans, wax beans and kidney beans. Add onion rings and green pepper. Heat, covered, for 5 minutes, until warm. Serve to accompany cold sliced turkey.

Serves 4.

five-minute harvard beets

two 16-ounce cans julienne beets
2 tablespoons butter or margarine
2 tablespoons flour
2 tablespoons sugar
¼ cup lemon juice
1 teaspoon salt

1. Drain juice from julienne beets. Set juice and beets aside.

2. Melt butter or margarine in medium saucepan over low heat; stir in flour and cook for 30 seconds, stirring constantly.

3. Slowly blend in beet juice, stirring constantly to keep smooth; bring to boiling point. Add beets; heat for 2 minutes. Stir in sugar, lemon juice and salt. Serve immediately.

Serves 4.

potato salad, two ways

2 pounds medium potatoes
8 slices bacon, cut into 1-inch pieces
1 cup finely chopped onion
1 cup finely chopped celery
1 cup cider vinegar
1 teaspoon sugar
½ teaspoon paprika

1. Peel potatoes and cut into ¼-inch-thick slices. Place in large saucepan with salted water to cover; simmer over medium heat until tender, about 10 minutes. Drain well and cool. Place half of potatoes in bowl. Set aside remaining potatoes.

2. Fry bacon in large skillet over medium heat until edges begin to curl. Add onion and celery; sauté until crisp-tender, about 3 minutes, stirring constantly. Stir in sugar and paprika. Pour half of mixture over potatoes in bowl.

3. Add remaining potatoes to dressing in skillet. Stir gently to blend. Cover and heat mixture for 3 to 4 minutes, until potatoes are very hot; serve immediately.

To serve cold: Toss potatoes in bowl with dressing. Chill; serve in lettuce-lined salad bowl.

Each half serves 4.

peasant vegetables italian style

2 pounds medium potatoes
½ cup olive oil
2 cloves garlic, crushed
two 15½-ounce cans green
   beans, drained
¼ cup chopped parsley
¼ cup grated Parmesan cheese
1 teaspoon salt
¼ teaspoon pepper

1. Peel potatoes; cut into ½-inch-thick slices. Place in large saucepan with salted water to cover; simmer over medium heat until tender, about 15 minutes. Drain very well and cool.

2. Heat oil in large skillet over medium heat; add garlic and sauté for 1 minute. Add potatoes; toss well and sauté for 5 minutes.

3. Add drained green beans; toss to combine and sauté for 2 minutes, until very hot. Stir in parsley, grated cheese, salt and pepper; heat 2 minutes longer. Serve half of mixture hot, as a vegetable.

To serve cold: Cool and chill remaining vegetables. Just before serving as salad, toss with ¼ cup red wine vinegar.

Each half serves 4.

ratatouille

⅓ cup olive oil
2 cloves garlic, slivered
1 medium eggplant, cubed
2 medium zucchini, sliced
1 cup chopped onion
4 medium tomatoes, coarsely
   chopped
½ cup sliced pitted black olives
1½ teaspoons salt
1 teaspoon oregano
¼ teaspoon pepper
¼ cup red wine vinegar

1. Heat oil in 3-quart heatproof casserole or saucepan over medium heat; add garlic and brown, then discard. Add eggplant, zucchini and onion to oil in pan.

2. Cook, covered, until vegetables are fork-tender, about 15 minutes, stirring occasionally. Stir in tomatoes, olives, salt, oregano and pepper; cook 5 minutes longer.

3. Stir in vinegar. Heat 2 minutes longer. Serve half of Ratatouille hot as a vegetable to accompany ham, pork or poultry.

To serve cold: Cool and chill remaining Ratatouille. Serve as a vegetable salad or relish to accompany chicken.

Each half serves 4.

chinese steak salad (*page 50*)

stuffed roast pork (*page 13*)

new york reuben sandwiches (*page 44*)

skillet chicken orange (*page 56*)

ribs, kraut and dumplings (*page 80*)

stir-fried chinese vegetables (*page 106*)

seafood chowder (*page 118*)

upside-down peach kuchen (*page 132*)

skillet vegetables

one 29-ounce can small whole potatoes

2 tablespoons butter or margarine

1 teaspoon garlic salt

¼ teaspoon pepper

one 16-ounce can zucchini, drained

1 cup grated mozzarella cheese

1. Rinse canned potatoes well under cold running water; pat dry with paper towels. Cut potatoes into ¼-inch slices.

2. Melt butter or margarine in medium skillet over medium heat; add potatoes, stirring to coat well with melted butter. Sprinkle with garlic salt and pepper.

3. Place zucchini over potatoes in an even layer; cover and cook for 10 minutes or until very hot. Sprinkle with grated cheese; cover again and cook until cheese is melted, about 3 to 4 minutes.

Serves 4.

hot-cold tomato soup

4 medium tomatoes

1 cup chopped pared cucumber

⅔ cup chopped green pepper

⅔ cup chopped onion

4 cups tomato juice

½ cup red wine vinegar

¼ cup olive or vegetable oil

2 envelopes beef powder concentrate

1 tablespoon Worcestershire sauce

½ teaspoon hot pepper sauce

garlic-flavored croutons

1. Peel tomatoes by plunging into boiling water for 1 minute; cool in cold water and remove and discard skins. Chop tomatoes coarsely. Place in blender container together with chopped cucumber, green pepper and onion. Add 2 cups of the tomato juice. Blend at high speed to puree vegetables, about 15 to 20 seconds.

2. Pour into large bowl; stir in remaining tomato juice, the vinegar, oil, beef concentrate, Worcestershire sauce and hot pepper sauce.

3. Pour 4 cups of the tomato mixture into medium saucepan. Heat until very hot but do not boil. Serve with garlic-flavored croutons.

To serve cold: Chill remaining soup; add a little more tomato juice if soup thickens. Serve with garlic-flavored croutons.

Each half serves 4.

ⓒ *EnergySaving Tip:* Bake homemade croutons in the oven—no matter what the temperature—while other dishes are cooking, or let the croutons crisp in the residual heat of the oven after other dishes have come out. To make croutons, spread both sides of day-old bread with seasoned butter or margarine and cut the bread into small cubes. Bake the bread cubes until they're crisp and dry, then store them in an airtight container to have on hand for casseroles and salads.

easy potato soup

2 tablespoons butter or margarine

¾ cup finely sliced green onions

two 10¾-ounce cans cream of potato soup

1½ cups light cream or half-and-half

1 cup sour cream

2 tablespoons lemon juice

2 teaspoons grated lemon rind

freshly ground black pepper

1. Melt butter or margarine in medium saucepan over low heat; add green onions and sauté until tender, about 3 to 4 minutes, stirring constantly.

2. Stir in potato soup and cream or half-and-half; heat to boiling point. Remove from heat; beat in sour cream, lemon juice and grated lemon rind.

3. Return to heat; heat until very hot but do not boil. Serve half of soup in individual serving bowls, grinding black pepper over each.

To serve cold: Cool and chill. If soup thickens, beat in a little more cream or half-and-half. Serve with freshly ground black pepper.

Each half serves 4.

PRESSURE COOKER

swiss steak

2-pound round steak, 1 inch thick

¼ cup flour

¼ cup butter or margarine

½ cup chopped onion

½ cup chopped celery

½ cup chopped green pepper

one 10¾-ounce can tomato soup

½ cup water

1 tablespoon Worcestershire sauce

¼ cup chopped parsley

1. Wipe round steak with damp paper towels; cut meat into 4 pieces. Sprinkle both sides of steak pieces with flour.

2. Melt butter or margarine in 4-quart pressure cooker over medium heat; add steak pieces and brown, about 2 minutes per side. Remove from pressure cooker; set aside.

3. Add onion, celery and green pepper to drippings in cooker; sauté for 2 minutes, stirring constantly. Stir in tomato soup, water and Worcestershire sauce. Place browned meat on top of vegetables.

4. Tightly secure lid on pressure cooker. Increase pressure, following manufacturer's instructions. Cook beef at 15 pounds pressure for 30 minutes. Cool as directed before removing lid.

5. Lift meat from pan juices to serving platter. Stir liquid well and pour over meat; sprinkle with parsley.

Serves 4.

beef roulades

2-pound round steak, 1 inch
    thick
½ cup dry red wine
2 tablespoons vegetable oil
¼ pound bacon, diced
½ cup chopped onion
12 stuffed green olives
1 cup beef broth
1 teaspoon salt
½ teaspoon thyme

1. Using very sharp knife, cut steak horizontally in half. Cut each slice in half; place between two sheets of waxed paper. Using wooden mallet or rolling pin, pound each slice until ¼ inch thick.

2. In large shallow baking dish, mix wine and oil. Add beef slices, turning to coat well. Cover and chill for at least 2 hours.

3. Sauté bacon and onion in 4-quart pressure cooker over medium heat until bacon is crisp and onion is brown, about 5 to 6 minutes, stirring constantly. Remove bacon and onion from pressure cooker with slotted spoon.

4. Remove meat from marinade; reserve marinade. Place 1-inch-wide band of bacon-onion mixture at one end of each beef slice. Place 3 olives across each band of stuffing.

5. Roll up beef slices jelly-roll fashion; secure with toothpicks. Sauté beef rolls in bacon fat remaining in pressure cooker for about 5 minutes, turning to brown all sides. Add reserved marinade, beef broth, salt and thyme.

6. Tightly secure lid on pressure cooker. Increase pressure, following manufacturer's instructions. Cook beef at 15 pounds pressure for 15 minutes. Cool as directed before removing lid.

7. Lift beef roulades from pan liquid to serving platter. Skim surface fat from pan liquid before serving alongside as gravy.

Serves 4.

◎ *EnergySaving Tip:* Meat that has been tenderized will cook more quickly, thus saving energy. You can tenderize veal or chicken cutlets by putting them between two sheets of waxed paper and pounding them with a wooden mallet or rolling pin until they're about ¼ inch thick. Marinating will tenderize any cut. Place the meat in a wine-oil mixture for the length of time specified in the recipe. Overnight marinating in the refrigerator will tenderize tougher cuts; turn the meat as often as possible while it marinates. If you prefer, you can substitute apple cider vinegar for wine in a marinade.

cantonese short ribs

¼ cup butter or margarine

3 pounds beef short ribs, cut into serving pieces

2 tablespoons soy sauce

1 cup chopped onion

½ cup chili sauce

½ cup dry red wine

¼ cup brown sugar, firmly packed

1 tablespoon prepared spicy mustard

one 8-ounce can water chestnuts, drained and sliced

one 4-ounce can button mushrooms, drained

1. Melt butter or margarine in 4-quart pressure cooker over medium heat; add beef ribs a few at a time and sauté for about 5 minutes, turning to brown all sides. Transfer ribs as browned to shallow pan; sprinkle with soy sauce.

2. Add onion to drippings in cooker; sauté until golden, about 4 minutes. Stir in chili sauce, wine, brown sugar and mustard. Return ribs to cooker; turn in sauce to coat well.

3. Tightly secure lid on pressure cooker. Increase pressure, following manufacturer's instructions. Cook beef ribs at 15 pounds pressure for 30 minutes. Cool as directed before removing lid.

4. Stir in drained water chestnuts and mushrooms; cook over low heat for 2 minutes to heat through.

Serves 4.

oniony beef short ribs

3 pounds beef short ribs, cut into serving pieces

2 tablespoons vegetable oil

1½ teaspoons salt

½ teaspoon pepper

2 cups sliced onions

1 cup sliced celery

one 15-ounce can tomato puree

1 cup beef broth

2 tablespoons flour

¼ cup water

chopped celery leaves

1. Wipe short ribs with damp paper towels. Heat oil in 4-quart pressure cooker over medium heat; add ribs a few at a time and sauté for about 5 minutes, turning to brown all sides. Remove ribs as browned and set aside.

2. Return all meat to pressure cooker. Sprinkle with salt and pepper. Add onions and celery; stir to combine. Pour in tomato puree and beef broth.

3. Tightly secure lid on pressure cooker. Increase pressure, following manufacturer's instructions. Cook at 15 pounds pressure for 30 minutes. Cool as directed before removing lid.

4. In small custard cup, blend flour and water. Stir into beef-vegetable mixture. Bring to boiling point over low heat, stirring constantly. Sprinkle with chopped celery leaves just before serving.

Serves 4.

speedy stuffed peppers

1 cup uncooked long-grain rice

4 large green peppers

¼ cup butter or margarine

1 cup chopped onion

1 clove garlic, crushed

1 pound ground beef

¼ cup brown sugar, firmly packed

1 egg, beaten

one 15½-ounce jar spaghetti sauce with mushrooms

1. Cook rice according to label directions. Meanwhile, cut ½-inch slice from top of each green pepper. Using a teaspoon, remove and discard seeds and membranes. Wash peppers well.

2. Melt butter or margarine in 4-quart pressure cooker over medium heat; add onion and garlic and sauté until onion is soft, about 3 to 4 minutes. Add ground beef and sauté for 5 minutes or until brown, stirring constantly. Remove mixture from cooker with slotted spoon; place in large bowl.

3. Add cooked rice, brown sugar and beaten egg to onion-beef mixture. Stuff green peppers with mixture. Stand stuffed peppers upright in cooker. Pour spaghetti sauce over and around peppers.

4. Tightly secure lid on pressure cooker. Increase pressure, following manufacturer's instructions. Cook peppers at 15 pounds pressure for 10 minutes. Cool as directed before removing lid. Place peppers on serving platter; pour remaining sauce from cooker over peppers.

Serves 4.

beef barley soup

2 tablespoons butter or margarine

½ pound ground beef

1 cup diced potato

½ cup diced carrot

½ cup chopped onion

½ cup chopped celery

1¾ cups water

one 8-ounce can tomato sauce

¼ cup pearl barley

1 teaspoon salt

½ teaspoon thyme

¼ cup chopped celery leaves

1. Melt butter or margarine in 4-quart pressure cooker over medium heat; add ground beef and sauté for 2 minutes. Add potato, carrot, onion and celery and sauté for 5 minutes or until tender, stirring constantly. Stir in water, tomato sauce, barley, salt and thyme.

2. Tightly secure lid on pressure cooker. Increase pressure, following manufacturer's instructions. Cook soup at 15 pounds pressure for 15 minutes. Cool as directed before removing lid. Sprinkle with chopped celery leaves.

Serves 4.

corned beef and cabbage

3- to 4-pound corned beef brisket

1 large onion

6 peppercorns

6 cloves

1 clove garlic, crushed

1 bay leaf

2 cups water

1 small head cabbage, quartered

1. Wipe corned beef very well with damp paper towels. Place meat on trivet or small wire rack in 4-quart pressure cooker.

2. Stud onion with peppercorns and cloves; place in cooker. Add garlic, bay leaf and water.

3. Tightly secure lid on pressure cooker. Increase pressure, following manufacturer's instructions. Cook beef at 15 pounds pressure for 45 minutes. Cool as directed before removing lid.

4. Place cabbage quarters around beef; tightly secure lid on pressure cooker once more. Return to 15 pounds pressure; cook 5 minutes longer. Cool once more as directed before removing lid.

5. Place beef and cabbage on serving platter; serve with horseradish or mustard.

Serves 8.

veal paprika

1½-pound veal steak

½ cup flour

2 tablespoons mild paprika

1 egg

1 tablespoon water

¼ cup butter or margarine

½ cup chicken broth

one 3-ounce can sliced mushrooms

1 teaspoon grated lemon rind

1 cup sour cream

1. Wipe veal with damp paper towels; cut meat into 4 pieces.

2. Blend together flour and paprika; place on plate. Beat together egg and water; pour onto second plate. Dip each meat piece into flour mixture to coat both sides. Dip into egg mixture, then once more into flour mixture to coat completely.

3. Melt butter or margarine in 4-quart pressure cooker over medium heat; add veal and brown, about 2 minutes per side. Add chicken broth, undrained mushrooms and grated lemon rind.

4. Tightly secure lid on pressure cooker. Increase pressure, following manufacturer's instructions. Cook veal at 15 pounds pressure for 15 minutes. Cool as directed before removing lid.

5. Lift meat to serving platter. Stir sour cream into pan juices; heat for 2 minutes but do not boil. Pour over veal steaks.

Serves 4.

lamb and onion curry

2 pounds lamb shoulder, cut into ¾-inch cubes

¼ cup flour

¼ cup butter or margarine

1 cup sliced onion

1 cup diced, peeled tart apple

1 clove garlic, crushed

2 tablespoons curry powder

1 teaspoon salt

1 cup beef broth

1 tablespoon cornstarch

1. Toss lamb cubes in flour to coat. Melt butter or margarine in 4-quart pressure cooker over medium heat; add lamb cubes a few at a time and sauté, turning to brown all sides. Remove lamb as browned and set aside.

2. Add onion, apple and garlic to drippings in cooker; sauté until onion and apple are soft, about 2 to 3 minutes. Stir in curry, salt and beef broth. Return meat to cooker; stir to mix well.

3. Tightly secure lid on pressure cooker. Increase pressure, following manufacturer's instructions. Cook curry at 15 pounds pressure for 15 minutes. Cool as directed before removing lid.

4. Blend cornstarch with a little water; stir into curry and bring to boiling point over low heat.

Serves 4.

creole pork chops

4 pork shoulder chops, ¾ inch thick

2 tablespoons butter or margarine

½ cup uncooked long-grain rice

1 cup chopped onion

½ cup chopped green pepper

one 20-ounce can whole tomatoes

1 tablespoon molasses

1 teaspoon coriander, or 1 tablespoon chopped parsley

1 teaspoon salt

1. Wipe pork chops well with damp paper towels. Melt butter or margarine in 4-quart pressure cooker over medium heat; add chops and brown, about 2 to 3 minutes per side. Remove from cooker and set aside.

2. Add rice to drippings in cooker; sauté until golden, about 2 to 3 minutes, stirring constantly. Reduce heat to low; add onion and green pepper and sauté 2 minutes longer.

3. Stir in tomatoes, molasses, coriander or parsley and salt; mix well, breaking tomatoes into small pieces. Return pork chops to cooker.

4. Tightly secure lid on pressure cooker. Increase pressure, following manufacturer's instructions. Cook pork chops at 15 pounds pressure for 20 minutes. Cool as directed before removing lid.

Serves 4.

ribs, kraut and dumplings

3 pounds spareribs, cut into serving pieces

2 tablespoons butter or margarine

½ cup chopped onion

two 16-ounce cans or packages sauerkraut

1 cup chopped, peeled tart apple

2 tablespoons brown sugar

1 teaspoon caraway seeds

2 cups packaged biscuit mix

⅔ cup milk

¼ cup chopped parsley

1. Wipe spareribs well with damp paper towels. Melt butter or margarine in 4-quart pressure cooker over medium heat; add sparerib pieces a few at a time and sauté, turning to brown all sides. Remove ribs as browned and set aside.

2. Add onion to drippings in cooker; sauté until golden, about 4 minutes. Add undrained sauerkraut, apple, brown sugar and caraway seeds; stir to mix well. Return ribs to cooker.

3. Tightly secure lid on pressure cooker. Increase pressure, following manufacturer's instructions. Cook spareribs at 15 pounds pressure for 20 minutes. Cool as directed before removing lid.

4. Meanwhile, combine biscuit mix, milk and parsley, stirring just until soft dough forms. Drop dough by tablespoonfuls on top of ribs and sauerkraut. Steam, covered, over low heat without pressure for 10 minutes or until dumplings are light and fluffy.

Serves 4. Shown on page 69.

savory ham balls with pineapple

one 20-ounce can pineapple chunks

4 cups ground precooked ham

¾ cup dry unseasoned bread crumbs

¼ cup apricot preserves

2 tablespoons soy sauce

1 egg, beaten

¼ cup butter or margarine

⅓ cup brown sugar, firmly packed

¼ cup cider vinegar

1 tablespoon dry mustard

1. Drain pineapple chunks, reserving juice to measure ¾ cup (add water if necessary). Set juice and pineapple aside.

2. In large bowl, combine ground ham, bread crumbs, apricot preserves, soy sauce and beaten egg. Shape ham into 36 balls, each ¾ inch in diameter.

3. Melt butter or margarine in 4-quart pressure cooker over medium heat; add meatballs a few at a time and sauté, turning to brown all sides. Remove from cooker as browned, then return all meatballs to cooker.

4. In small bowl, blend brown sugar, vinegar and dry mustard. Spoon over meatballs; pour ¼ cup of the reserved pineapple juice into pressure cooker.

5. Tightly secure lid on pressure cooker. Increase pressure, following maufacturer's instructions. Cook meatballs at 15 pounds pressure for 20 minutes. Cool as directed before removing lid.

6. Remove meatballs from pan liquid with slotted spoon; place on serving platter. Add remaining pineapple juice and the pineapple chunks to pressure cooker. Simmer over low heat for 2 to 3 minutes. Spoon over meatballs.

Serves 4.

pressure-barbecued chicken

2½- to 3-pound broiler-fryer chicken, cut into serving pieces
¼ cup flour
¼ cup butter or margarine
½ cup chopped onion
½ cup brown sugar, firmly packed
½ cup ketchup
½ cup cider vinegar
½ teaspoon salt

1. Wash chicken pieces well under cold running water; pat dry with paper towels. Place chicken in large, clean brown paper or plastic bag along with flour; shake to coat well.

2. Melt butter or margarine in 4-quart pressure cooker over medium heat; add chicken pieces a few at a time and sauté, turning to brown all sides. Remove pieces as browned and set aside.

3. Add onion to drippings in cooker; sauté until golden, about 4 minutes, stirring constantly. Stir in brown sugar, ketchup, vinegar and salt. Return chicken to pressure cooker; turn chicken in sauce to coat well.

4. Tightly secure lid on pressure cooker. Increase pressure, following manufacturer's instructions. Cook chicken at 15 pounds pressure for 15 minutes. Cool as directed before removing lid. Gently turn chicken in sauce before placing on serving platter.

Serves 4.

◎ *EnergySaving Tip:* Use the cooking liquid remaining in your pressure cooker as a sauce base for the meat you've been cooking. Just stir in some cornstarch (about 1 tablespoon for 1½ to 2 cups liquid) that's been blended with a little cold water, and heat the mixture for 30 to 60 seconds to thicken it. This avoids using extra energy to melt fat, cook flour or bring a cold liquid to the boiling point.

chicken soup

2½- to 3-pound broiler-fryer chicken, cut into serving pieces

¼ cup butter or margarine

½ cup finely diced onion

½ cup finely diced carrot

½ cup finely diced potato

two 1½-ounce packages chicken-rice soup mix

6 cups water

1. Wash chicken well under cold running water; pat dry with paper towels. Melt butter or margarine in 4-quart pressure cooker over medium heat; add chicken pieces a few at a time and sauté, turning to brown all sides. Remove chicken as browned and set aside.

2. Add onion, carrot and potato to drippings in cooker; sauté until onion is golden, about 5 minutes. Stir in chicken-rice soup mix and water. Return chicken pieces to pressure cooker.

3. Tightly secure lid on pressure cooker. Increase pressure, following manufacturer's instructions. Cook soup at 15 pounds pressure for 15 minutes. Cool as directed before removing lid. Lift chicken from soup; cut meat from bones, dice and return to soup.

Serves 4 to 6.

boston "baked" beans

1 pound dried pea beans

½ pound bacon, diced

½ cup chopped onion

¼ cup dark brown sugar, firmly packed

¼ cup molasses

¼ cup ketchup

1 tablespoon prepared spicy mustard

cold water

1. Wash beans under cold running water; discard any imperfect beans or debris. Place beans in medium saucepan; add water twice the depth of beans in pan. Bring to boiling point over medium heat; boil 1 minute. Cool beans and soak overnight.

2. Fry bacon in 4-quart pressure cooker over medium heat until semi-crisp; add onion and sauté until golden, about 4 minutes, stirring constantly.

3. Drain water from beans; add beans to pressure cooker (do not drain any fat from cooker). Stir in molasses, ketchup and mustard; mix well. Add enough cold water to cover beans.

4. Tightly secure lid on pressure cooker. Increase pressure, following manufacturer's instructions. Cook beans at 15 pounds pressure for 40 minutes. Cool as directed before removing lid. Stir well.

Serves 4.

EnergySaving Tip: For a long time it was thought that bean dishes couldn't be made successfully in the energy-efficient pressure cooker; the secret is to use the correct amount of fat, as specified in these recipes. Another thing to remember when making these bean dishes is to clean the vent very well before making any other dish in the pressure cooker.

dutch lima beans

1 pound dried lima beans
½ pound herb-seasoned sausages, cut into ½-inch slices
1 cup chopped onion
¾ cup unsweetened apple juice
½ cup ketchup
2 tablespoons brown sugar
1 teaspoon salt
1 teaspoon prepared spicy mustard

1. Wash beans under cold running water; discard any imperfect beans or debris. Place beans in medium saucepan; add water twice the depth of beans in pan. Bring water to boiling point over medium heat; boil 1 minute. Cool beans and soak overnight.

2. Sauté sausage slices in 4-quart pressure cooker over medium heat until brown, about 5 to 8 minutes, stirring constantly. Remove sausages with slotted spoon; set aside.

3. Pour all but ¼ cup drippings from cooker; add onion to drippings in cooker and sauté over medium heat until tender, about 5 minutes, stirring constantly.

4. Drain water from lima beans; add beans to pressure cooker along with browned sausage slices. Stir in apple juice, ketchup, brown sugar, salt and mustard.

5. Tightly secure lid on pressure cooker. Increase pressure, following manufacturer's instructions. Cook beans at 15 pounds pressure for 30 minutes. Cool as directed before removing lid. Stir well.

Serves 4.

cauliflower cheese

1 medium head cauliflower
½ cup milk
½ teaspoon salt
1 cup grated sharp Cheddar cheese
3 to 4 drops hot pepper sauce
¼ cup slivered almonds
1 teaspoon mild paprika

1. Trim green leaves from cauliflower. Wash cauliflower under cold running water; drain well. Place on trivet or small wire rack in 4-quart pressure cooker; add milk and salt.

2. Tightly secure lid on pressure cooker. Increase pressure, following manufacturer's instructions. Cook cauliflower at 15 pounds pressure for 5 minutes. Cool as directed before removing lid. Place cauliflower in serving dish; keep warm.

3. Drain all but ⅓ cup cooking liquid from cooker; remove trivet. Add cheese and hot pepper sauce to liquid in cooker.

4. Cook over low heat until cheese is melted, about 3 to 4 minutes, stirring constantly. Spoon over cauliflower; sprinkle with slivered almonds and paprika.

Serves 4.

sweet potato crescents

3 medium-size sweet potatoes

½ cup water

½ cup brown sugar, firmly packed

1 medium orange

1 egg

1 tablespoon water

1 cup crushed cornflakes

½ cup butter or margarine

1. Wash sweet potatoes very well; cut lengthwise in half. Place cut side up on trivet or small wire rack in 4-quart pressure cooker. Add ½ cup water.

2. Tightly secure lid on pressure cooker. Increase pressure, following manufacturer's instructions. Cook sweet potatoes at 15 pounds pressure for 8 minutes. Cool as directed before removing lid. When potatoes are cool enough to handle, peel off skin; mash potatoes with brown sugar.

3. Using small sharp knife, cut skin from orange; cut orange into segments. Mold mashed sweet potatoes around orange segments to form crescents.

4. Beat egg with 1 tablespoon water; pour onto plate. Place crushed cornflakes on second plate. Dip crescents into beaten egg and then into crumbs to coat. Chill for 15 minutes to set coating.

5. Remove trivet from cooker. Melt butter or margarine in cooker over medium heat; add crescents and sauté for about 3 minutes, turning to brown all sides.

Makes approximately 12 crescents; serves 4.

apple brown betty

1½ cups dry unseasoned bread crumbs

⅓ cup butter or margarine, melted

⅓ cup brown sugar, firmly packed

2 tablespoons lemon juice

1 teaspoon grated lemon rind

½ teaspoon nutmeg

¼ teaspoon cinnamon

4 medium-size tart cooking apples, cored, peeled and sliced

1. Generously grease 1½-quart ovenproof bowl that fits easily into 4-quart pressure cooker; set aside.

2. In medium bowl, toss together bread crumbs, melted butter or margarine, brown sugar, lemon juice, grated lemon rind, nutmeg and cinnamon.

3. Place 1 cup of the sliced apples in bottom of greased bowl; top with one-fourth of crumb mixture; arrange 3 more layers of apples and crumb mixture, ending with layer of crumbs.

4. Tightly cover top of bowl with waxed paper and foil; secure in place with string. Place on trivet or small wire rack in 4-quart pressure cooker. Add 1 cup water to cooker.

5. Tightly secure lid on pressure cooker. Increase pressure, following manufacturer's instructions. Cook pudding at 15 pounds pressure for 15 minutes. Cool as directed before removing lid.

6. Let pudding cool at room temperature before serving. Serve with ice cream if desired.

Serves 4.

steamed cottage pudding

1½ cups cubed day-old bread

½ cup snipped dates or chopped raisins

½ cup chopped nuts

⅓ cup brown sugar, firmly packed

¼ teaspoon cinnamon

¼ teaspoon nutmeg

3 cups milk

2 eggs, beaten

1 tablespoon vanilla extract

1. Generously grease 1½-quart ovenproof bowl that fits easily into 4-quart pressure cooker.

2. In greased bowl, combine bread cubes, dates or raisins, nuts, brown sugar, cinnamon and nutmeg; toss to mix well.

3. Heat milk in medium saucepan until lukewarm; remove from heat. Rapidly beat in beaten eggs and vanilla extract. Pour over bread-fruit mixture; let stand for 2 minutes.

4. Tightly cover top of bowl with waxed paper and foil; secure in place with string. Place bowl on trivet or small wire rack in 4-quart pressure cooker. Add 4 cups water to cooker, or enough to come halfway up side of bowl.

5. Tightly secure lid on pressure cooker. Increase pressure, following manufacturer's instructions. Cook pudding at 15 pounds pressure for 20 minutes. Cool as directed before removing lid. Let pudding cool at room temperature for 10 minutes before serving.

Serves 4.

indian pudding

4 cups milk

1 cup yellow cornmeal

½ cup dark molasses

⅓ cup sugar

2 tablespoons butter or margarine

2 teaspoons ginger

½ teaspoon salt

1. Scald 3 cups of the milk in top of double boiler over medium heat. In small bowl, blend cornmeal and remaining milk; stir cornmeal mixture into scalded milk.

2. Place top of double boiler over boiling water; cook until mixture is thickened, about 10 to 15 minutes, stirring constantly. Remove from heat; beat in molasses, sugar, butter or margarine, ginger and salt.

3. Generously grease 1½-quart ovenproof bowl that fits easily into 4-quart pressure cooker. Pour thickened cornmeal mixture into bowl. Tightly cover top of bowl with waxed paper and foil; secure in place with string. Place bowl on trivet or small wire rack in pressure cooker. Add 1 cup water to cooker.

4. Tightly secure lid on pressure cooker. Increase pressure, following manufacturer's instructions. Cook pudding at 15 pounds pressure for 15 minutes. Cool as directed before removing lid.

5. Let pudding cool at room temperature before serving. Serve with pouring cream if desired.

Serves 4.

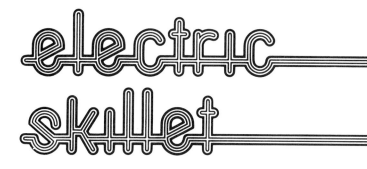

electric skillet

The marvel of many modern appliances is their wide range of uses in food preparation. Electric skillets are in this class of kitchen equipment. They can gently sauté Scrambled Eggs and Mushrooms, simmer Skillet Stroganoff or turn out Quick Fried Rice and Ham. Some are even equipped with high-domed lids, which permit the roasting of meats. But lately electric skillets have been standing in for a very old but new-to-America kitchen tool—the wok, the traditional stir-fry utensil that comes from China.

The Chinese have used the energy-efficient stir-fry method of cooking for thousands of years. There's nothing exotic about it; it's a simple technique in which foods are fried briefly over intense heat, rendering them crisp-tender and keeping their nutrients intact. The greatest expenditure of energy in stir-frying is actually yours: stir-fried foods are first prepared by slicing, chopping, mincing and marinating. Even if there's a strictly meat-and-potatoes crew at your house, try stir-frying some Steak and Peppers for dinner or slipping in a Savory Chinese Omelet one Sunday morning—your family will be glad you did.

Whether it's beef, chicken, pork, fish or vegetables you desire, there are fabulous recipes for you in the following pages.

steak and peppers

1 pound round steak, cut into
2½ x ¼-inch strips

⅓ cup vegetable oil

3 tablespoons red wine vinegar

1 clove garlic, crushed

½ teaspoon salt

¼ teaspoon pepper

2 cups julienne strips green
pepper

1 cup thinly sliced onion

2 tablespoons soy sauce

1. In shallow glass baking dish, combine beef strips, oil, vinegar, garlic, salt and pepper. Chill for at least 8 hours; stir frequently. Remove beef from marinade; reserve marinade.

2. Brown beef strips in electric skillet at medium heat. Add green pepper and onion; cook for 2 minutes, stirring constantly.

3. Add marinade and soy sauce to skillet; stir to combine well. Reduce heat to low and simmer until pepper and onion are just tender, about 5 minutes, stirring constantly.

Serves 4.

forty-minute beef stew

1½ pounds round steak, cut
into ¾-inch cubes

¼ cup flour

1 teaspoon salt

½ teaspoon pepper

2 tablespoons butter or
margarine

1 cup chopped onion

1 envelope beef powder
concentrate

1¼ cups water

1 cup julienne strips carrots

1 cup sour cream

1 tablespoon horseradish,
drained

1. In large, clean brown paper or plastic bag, toss beef cubes in mixture of flour, salt and pepper to coat well. Set aside.

2. Melt butter or margarine in electric skillet at medium heat; add beef cubes a few at a time and sauté, turning to brown all sides. Remove meat as browned and set aside.

3. Add onion to drippings in skillet; sauté until golden, about 4 minutes, stirring constantly. Return beef cubes to skillet; stir in beef concentrate and water.

4. Reduce heat to low and simmer, covered, for 10 minutes. Add carrots; cover and simmer 20 minutes longer or until beef and carrots are tender.

5. Stir in sour cream and drained horseradish; heat until very hot but do not boil.

Serves 4.

beef stew french style

1½ pounds sirloin or chuck
  beef, cut into 2 x ¼-inch strips
¼ cup flour
2 teaspoons salt
¼ teaspoon nutmeg
¼ cup butter or margarine
¼ cup vegetable oil
1 cup julienne strips green
  pepper
2 cups sliced mushrooms
1 cup thinly sliced carrots
1 cup dry red wine
1 cup unflavored yogurt
½ cup chopped parsley

1. Toss beef strips in mixture of flour, salt and nutmeg to coat. Heat 2 tablespoons of the butter or margarine and 2 tablespoons of the oil in electric skillet at medium heat; add beef strips a few at a time and sauté until golden brown. Remove meat as browned and set aside.

2. Heat remaining butter or margarine and oil in skillet at medium heat; add green pepper strips, mushrooms and carrots and sauté until tender, about 5 minutes.

3. Return meat to skillet; add wine. Reduce heat to low and simmer, covered, until meat is tender, about 20 to 30 minutes.

4. Blend in yogurt and parsley; heat, but do not boil, 3 minutes longer, stirring constantly.

Serves 4.

skillet stroganoff

1½ pounds sirloin or chuck
  beef, cut into 2 x ¼-inch strips
¼ cup flour
½ cup butter or margarine
2 cups sliced mushrooms
1 cup chopped onion
one 10½-ounce can beef
  bouillon
1 cup tomato juice
½ cup dry sherry
½ cup sour cream

1. Toss beef strips in flour to coat. Melt ¼ cup of the butter or margarine in electric skillet at medium heat; add beef strips a few at a time and sauté until golden brown. Remove meat as browned and set aside.

2. Melt remaining butter or margarine in skillet; add mushrooms and onion and sauté until tender, about 8 to 10 minutes, stirring constantly.

3. Add beef bouillon, tomato juice and sherry to skillet; bring to boiling point, stirring constantly. Return meat to skillet. Reduce heat to low and simmer, covered, until meat is tender, about 20 to 30 minutes.

4. Blend in sour cream; heat, but do not boil, 3 minutes longer, stirring constantly.

Serves 4.

beef sukiyaki

¼ cup vegetable oil

1½ pounds beef sirloin, cut into
2 x ¼-inch strips

2 cloves garlic, crushed

1 cup sliced mushrooms

1 cup green onion strips (2-inch
pieces cut lengthwise in half)

one 5-ounce can bamboo
shoots, drained

¼ cup soy sauce

2 tablespoons brown sugar

½ teaspoon salt

¼ teaspoon pepper

1. Heat oil in electric skillet at medium heat; add beef strips and sauté until lightly browned, about 2 to 3 minutes.

2. Push meat to side of skillet; add mushrooms and green onions. Sauté for 2 to 3 minutes, stirring constantly; toss with meat. Add drained bamboo shoots; toss once more.

3. In small bowl, blend together soy sauce, brown sugar, salt and pepper. Pour over ingredients in skillet; increase heat to high and toss ingredients together for 2 minutes.

Serves 4.

chili and beans

1 tablespoon vegetable oil

1 pound ground beef

½ cup chopped onion

½ teaspoon salt

¼ teaspoon pepper

one 16-ounce can tomato
sauce

one 15½-ounce can kidney
beans, drained

2 teaspoons chili powder

½ cup grated Monterey Jack or
mozzarella cheese

one 11-ounce can tortillas

1. Heat oil in electric skillet at medium heat; add ground beef and brown for about 5 minutes, stirring constantly to break meat into small pieces.

2. Add onion, salt and pepper; cook 2 minutes longer, stirring constantly. Stir in tomato sauce, drained kidney beans and chili powder. Reduce heat to low and simmer, covered, for 15 to 20 minutes.

3. Sprinkle grated cheese over chili; heat, covered, for 1 minute to melt cheese. Serve over heated tortillas.

Serves 4.

EnergySaving Tip: You can easily melt cheese to top oven casseroles and skillet dishes without using any extra energy. No need to turn on the broiler—just sprinkle the grated or shredded cheese on top of the hot, cooked skillet dish or oven casserole and cover it briefly. The heat from the dish will do the job. An easy measurement guideline to keep in mind: ¼ pound (4 ounces) of cheese will yield 1 cup of grated or shredded cheese.

german skillet dinner

2 tablespoons butter or margarine

one 16-ounce can or package sauerkraut

½ cup uncooked long-grain rice

½ cup chopped onion

1 pound ground beef

½ teaspoon salt

¼ teaspoon pepper

one 8-ounce can tomato sauce

1. Melt butter or margarine in electric skillet at low heat; spread undrained sauerkraut over bottom of skillet.

2. Sprinkle rice and onion over sauerkraut. Crumble ground beef finely and sprinkle over rice-onion layer; sprinkle salt and pepper over beef.

3. Pour tomato sauce over beef layer. Simmer, covered, over low heat until meat is tender and ingredients are hot, 25 to 30 minutes.

Serves 4.

hungarian skillet supper

2 tablespoons butter or margarine

1 pound ground round beef

1 clove garlic, crushed

1 teaspoon paprika

½ teaspoon salt

¼ teaspoon pepper

1 envelope beef powder concentrate

one 16-ounce can tomato sauce

½ cup water

½ cup quick-cooking rice

2 cups finely shredded cabbage

1. Melt butter or margarine in electric skillet at medium heat; add ground beef and brown for about 5 minutes, stirring constantly to break meat into small pieces.

2. Add garlic, paprika, salt and pepper; cook for 1 minute, stirring constantly. Blend in beef concentrate, tomato sauce, water and rice. Reduce heat to low and simmer, covered, for 5 minutes or until rice is just tender.

3. Add cabbage; cover and cook 5 minutes longer, until cabbage is crisp-tender.

Serves 4.

dinnertime meatballs

1 pound ground beef
½ cup finely chopped onion
½ cup crushed cornflakes
¼ cup chopped parsley
1 clove garlic, crushed
1 teaspoon salt
¼ teaspoon pepper
1 egg
⅓ cup milk
2 tablespoons ketchup
2 tablespoons vegetable oil
1 tablespoon flour
1 cup beef broth

1. In large bowl, combine ground beef, onion, cornflakes, parsley, garlic, salt and pepper. In small bowl, beat together egg, milk and ketchup; add to ground beef mixture and mix to blend well. Shape into 1-inch meatballs.

2. Heat oil in electric skillet at low heat; add meatballs a few at a time and sauté for about 10 minutes, turning to brown all sides. Remove meatballs as browned and set aside

3. Pour all but 1 tablespoon drippings from skillet; add flour to drippings in skillet, stirring to loosen brown particles. Slowly add beef broth, stirring to keep mixture smooth.

4. Bring to boiling point over medium heat, stirring constantly until mixture thickens. Return meatballs to skillet; reduce heat to low and simmer, covered, for 10 minutes. Serve with cooked noodles or rice.

Serves 4.

savory meatballs

1½ pounds ground beef
1 cup fresh bread crumbs
½ cup finely chopped onion
1 clove garlic, crushed
1 teaspoon salt
¼ teaspoon pepper
1 egg, slightly beaten
¼ cup butter or margarine
one 16-ounce can whole
  cranberry sauce
one 16-ounce can tomato
  sauce

1. In large mixing bowl, blend ground beef, bread crumbs, onion, garlic, salt, pepper and slightly beaten egg. Shape mixture into 1-inch meatballs.

2. Melt butter or margarine in electric skillet at medium heat; add meatballs a few at a time and sauté for about 5 minutes, turning to brown all sides lightly. Remove meatballs as browned and set aside.

3. Pour drippings from skillet; melt cranberry sauce in skillet over low heat. Stir in tomato sauce.

4. Return meatballs to skillet, turning in sauce to coat well. Simmer, covered, until meatballs are tender, about 20 minutes.

Serves 4.

veal scallops french style

¼ cup butter or margarine, melted

8 veal scallops, pounded thin

4 thin slices precooked ham

⅓ cup flour

½ teaspoon salt

¼ teaspoon pepper

2 eggs

2 tablespoons water

¼ cup butter or margarine

⅓ cup Marsala wine

¼ cup herb-garlic-seasoned cream cheese

1. Brush some of the melted ¼ cup butter or margarine on one side of 4 veal scallops. Top each with a ham slice; brush with remaining melted butter or margarine. Top ham slices with remaining veal scallops. Chill for at least 30 minutes.

2. On large plate, combine flour, salt and pepper. Beat together eggs and water; pour onto second plate. Dip chilled scallops into flour; shake to remove surplus. Dip into beaten egg mixture to coat both sides; drain slightly and coat with flour once more. Chill veal scallops for 30 minutes.

3. Melt ¼ cup butter or margarine in electric skillet at medium heat; add veal scallops and sauté until golden brown, 2 minutes per side. Add Marsala wine; heat to simmering point. Top each scallop with 1 tablespoon cheese; cover skillet and heat just to melt cheese.

Serves 4.

pork alsace

4 pork cutlets, ¾ inch thick

¼ cup gin

¼ cup water

2 tablespoons bottled steak sauce

2 tablespoons red wine vinegar

½ teaspoon pepper

one 16-ounce can or package sauerkraut, rinsed and drained

1. Wipe pork cutlets with damp paper towels. In shallow glass baking dish, combine gin, water, steak sauce, vinegar and pepper. Add pork cutlets, turning to coat well with marinade. Cover and chill for at least 6 hours, turning cutlets from time to time. Remove cutlets from marinade; reserve marinade.

2. Trim a little fat from edge of each cutlet. Fry pork trimmings in electric skillet at medium heat to yield 2 tablespoons fat. Discard trimmings. Add pork cutlets to fat and brown, about 3 to 4 minutes per side.

3. Add sauerkraut and ¼ cup reserved marinade. Reduce heat to low and simmer, covered, for 20 to 25 minutes or until pork is tender.

Serves 4.

Note: Gin may be omitted; substitute ¼ cup water and 6 crushed juniper berries.

spicy supper pork

4 pork shoulder chops, ½ inch thick

6 small potatoes, peeled and cut into ¼-inch-thick slices

4 medium carrots, peeled and cut into julienne strips

one 10¾-ounce can tomato soup

½ cup beef broth

2 teaspoons Worcestershire sauce

½ teaspoon crushed basil

1. Trim a little fat from edge of each pork chop; place fat in electric skillet and melt at low heat to coat bottom of skillet. Increase heat to medium; add pork chops and sauté until golden brown, about 4 minutes per side. Remove from skillet and set aside.

2. Add potatoes and carrots to drippings in skillet; toss to coat with fat and sauté for 2 to 3 minutes. Gently shake skillet so potatoes and carrots form an even layer over bottom. Place meat on top of potatoes and carrots.

3. In medium bowl, blend together tomato soup, beef broth, Worcestershire sauce and basil; pour over pork chops. Simmer, covered, for 20 to 30 minutes, until pork is pale pink-white near bone and vegetables are tender.

Serves 4.

sausage and apple kraut

1 pound bulk sausage meat

1 cup thinly sliced apple

1 cup thin onion rings

one 16-ounce can or package sauerkraut, rinsed and drained

⅓ cup dry white wine

1 teaspoon caraway seeds

⅛ teaspoon pepper

1. Brown sausage meat in electric skillet at medium heat, stirring constantly to break meat into small pieces. Remove from skillet with slotted spoon; set aside.

2. Pour all but 2 tablespoons fat from skillet; add apples and onion rings to fat in skillet and sauté until tender, about 4 minutes.

3. Stir in sauerkraut, white wine, caraway seeds, pepper and browned sausage meat. Reduce heat to low and simmer, covered, for 5 minutes, stirring occasionally.

Serves 4.

sweet and hot sausage and peppers

¾ pound sweet Italian-style sausages

¾ pound hot Italian-style sausages

2 tablespoons butter or margarine

2 cups julienne strips green pepper

1 cup thinly sliced onion

½ teaspoon salt

¼ teaspoon pepper

1. Prick sausages thoroughly with fork. Place in electric skillet; add water to cover. Bring to simmering point at medium heat. Cook, covered, for 20 minutes. Remove from skillet and set aside.

2. Drain cooking liquid from skillet and wipe skillet with paper towels. Melt butter or margarine in skillet at medium heat; add sausages and sauté for about 5 minutes, turning to brown all sides.

3. Stir in green pepper strips, onion, salt and pepper; sauté until tender, about 5 minutes, stirring constantly.

Serves 4.

quick fried rice and ham

one 6¼-ounce package fried rice mix

½ cup thinly sliced green onions

¼ pound precooked ham, cut into julienne strips

one 4-ounce can sliced mushrooms, drained

1 tablespoon soy sauce

1. Prepare fried rice mix according to label directions in electric skillet, adding green onions before cooking.

2. Before frying, add ham and drained mushrooms. Sprinkle with soy sauce just before serving.

Serves 4.

monte carlo snackwiches

¼ cup butter or margarine, softened

16 slices white bread

2 tablespoons mayonnaise

1 tablespoon prepared mild mustard

two 6-ounce packages sliced Swiss cheese

8 slices precooked ham

4 eggs

½ cup milk

½ cup butter or margarine

1. Use ¼ cup softened butter or margarine to spread one side of each bread slice. Blend mayonnaise with mustard; spread on unbuttered side of bread slices.

2. Arrange 8 bread slices buttered side down on baking sheet; place cheese slice, ham slice and another cheese slice on each. Top with remaining bread slices, buttered side up.

3. Beat together eggs and milk; dip sandwiches in mixture. Melt ½ cup butter or margarine in electric skillet at medium heat; add sandwiches and fry on both sides until bread is golden brown and cheese is melted. Serve half of sandwiches as a snack.

DOUBLE BATCH

4. Place remaining cooked sandwiches on paper towels to drain and cool. Wrap individually in foil. Freeze up to 2 weeks.

5. To serve, place frozen sandwiches on baking sheet and reheat in 425° F oven for 15 to 20 minutes.

Each half serves 4.

chicken cacciatore

2½- to 3-pound broiler-fryer chicken, cut into serving pieces

⅓ cup flour

¼ cup vegetable oil

½ cup chopped onion

½ cup chopped green pepper

1 clove garlic, crushed

one 16-ounce can tomato sauce

one 6-ounce can tomato paste

½ cup dry white wine

1 teaspoon salt

¼ teaspoon pepper

¼ teaspoon basil

2 cups thinly sliced fresh mushrooms

1. Wash chicken under cold running water; pat dry with paper towels. Place flour in large, clean brown paper or plastic bag; shake chicken pieces, two at a time, in flour to coat.

2. Heat oil in electric skillet at medium heat; add chicken pieces and sauté for about 15 minutes, turning to brown all sides. Remove from skillet and set aside.

3. Add onion, green pepper and garlic to drippings in skillet; sauté until tender, about 4 minutes, stirring constantly. Stir in tomato sauce, tomato paste, wine, salt, pepper and basil.

4. Return chicken to skillet, turning in sauce to coat well. Add mushrooms. Reduce heat to low and simmer, covered, for 35 to 40 minutes, until chicken is tender.

Serves 4.

Note: If sauce becomes too thick during cooking, stir in a little additional wine.

Ⓢ *EnergySaving Tip:* If you've made Chicken Cacciatore or any other chicken stew and there's some left over, save the extras and conserve the energy of making soup from scratch. Remove and discard the chicken bones; puree the leftovers with some additional broth and/or wine in a blender or food processor. Serve the pureed mixture either hot or chilled for lunch or as a first course.

california chicken

4 chicken breast halves

one 6-ounce jar marinated artichoke hearts

one 10¾-ounce can cream of mushroom soup

one 8-ounce can tomato sauce

½ cup milk

½ teaspoon ground coriander

1. Wash chicken breast halves under cold running water; pat dry with paper towels.

2. Drain liquid from artichoke hearts into electric skillet. Cut artichokes into quarters and set aside. Place chicken skin side down in skillet; cook at medium heat until brown, about 5 minutes per side. Pour excess cooking liquid from skillet.

3. In medium bowl, blend mushroom soup, tomato sauce, milk and coriander. Stir in quartered artichoke hearts. Pour sauce over chicken. Simmer, covered, at low heat until chicken is tender, about 20 to 30 minutes.

Serves 4.

chicken piccata

4 chicken breast halves, skinned and boned

2 eggs

½ cup milk

1 cup dry seasoned bread crumbs

¼ cup chopped parsley

1 teaspoon salt

¼ teaspoon pepper

2 tablespoons vegetable oil

2 tablespoons butter or margarine

2 envelopes chicken powder concentrate

1 cup water

¾ cup dry white wine

¼ cup lemon juice

1. Wash chicken under cold running water; pat dry with paper towels. Place each chicken breast half between two sheets of waxed paper; using wooden mallet or rolling pin, pound until ¼ inch thick.

2. Beat together eggs and milk; pour onto large plate. Combine bread crumbs, parsley, salt and pepper; place on second plate. Dip chicken breasts into egg mixture; drain slightly. Dip into crumb mixture to coat both sides; chill for 30 minutes to firm coating.

3. Heat oil and butter or margarine in electric skillet at medium heat; add chicken breasts and sauté until golden brown, 2 minutes per side. Remove from skillet and drain on paper towels; keep warm.

4. Reduce heat to low; add chicken concentrate to drippings in skillet. Stir with wooden spoon to blend and loosen brown particles. Add water and wine; bring to boiling point at medium heat, stirring constantly. Reduce heat to low and simmer for 5 minutes.

5. Add lemon juice; heat but do not boil. Arrange chicken on serving platter; pour a little of the sauce over chicken and serve remaining sauce alongside.

Serves 4.

chicken san francisco

1 pound chicken breast halves, skinned and boned

⅓ cup soy sauce

¼ cup bottled herbed salad dressing

one 10-ounce package frozen chopped broccoli

½ cup thinly sliced celery

¼ cup thinly sliced green onion

1 envelope chicken powder concentrate

1. Wash chicken under cold running water; pat dry with paper towels. Cut into ¼-inch-thick strips. In shallow baking dish, combine soy sauce and herbed salad dressing. Add chicken strips, tossing well to coat. Cover and chill for 4 hours.

2. Cook chicken in marinade in electric skillet at medium heat until chicken turns white, stirring constantly.

3. Reduce heat to low; add broccoli, celery and onion. Simmer, covered, stirring occasionally, until vegetables are just tender. Sprinkle in chicken concentrate; cook 1 minute longer. Serve over cooked rice or rice and noodle mixture if desired.

Serves 4.

skillet sweet and sour chicken

2 whole chicken breasts, skinned and boned

2 tablespoons vegetable oil

1½ cups thin onion rings

1 cup thinly sliced carrots

1 cup thinly sliced celery

one 8½-ounce can pineapple tidbits, drained

one 8-ounce package frozen snow peas, thawed

SAUCE

2 tablespoons cornstarch

2 tablespoons sugar

½ teaspoon ginger

2 tablespoons soy sauce

2 tablespoons vinegar

one 10¾-ounce can chicken broth

1. Wash chicken breasts well under cold running water; pat dry with paper towels. Cut chicken into julienne strips, slicing across the grain of meat. Set aside.

2. Heat oil in electric skillet at medium heat; add chicken strips and onion rings and sauté until lightly browned, about 5 to 8 minutes.

3. Add carrots, celery, drained pineapple tidbits and snow peas; stir to combine well. Sauté for 3 to 4 minutes, stirring constantly.

4. To make sauce, blend cornstarch, sugar, ginger, soy sauce, vinegar and chicken broth in small bowl. Stir until smooth. Pour over mixture in skillet; bring to boiling point, stirring constantly until mixture thickens.

Serves 4.

sherried chicken livers

2 pounds chicken livers
4 slices bacon
2 tablespoons butter or margarine
2 cups thin onion rings
4 cups sliced fresh mushrooms, or one 8-ounce can sliced mushrooms, drained
½ cup dry sherry
1 tablespoon soy sauce
¼ cup chopped parsley

1. Wash chicken livers under cold running water; pat dry with paper towels. Cut livers in half, trimming away and discarding fat. Set chicken livers aside.

2. Fry bacon in electric skillet at medium heat until crisp, about 5 minutes. Drain bacon on paper towels; break into bite-size pieces and set aside.

3. Melt butter or margarine in bacon fat in skillet; add onion rings and sauté until tender, about 5 minutes, stirring constantly.

4. Add chicken livers and mushrooms; toss to blend with onion rings. Fry at high heat for 2 minutes, stirring constantly.

5. Reduce heat to low; add sherry and soy sauce. Cover and simmer until mushrooms are tender and chicken livers are tender and pink inside, about 5 minutes. Sprinkle with bacon and heat 1 minute longer. Just before serving, sprinkle with parsley.

Serves 4.

sole almondine

one 16-ounce package frozen fillets of sole, thawed
2 eggs, slightly beaten
¾ cup dry seasoned bread crumbs
3 tablespoons butter or margarine
¼ cup slivered blanched almonds
lemon wedges

1. Wipe fish fillets with damp paper towels. Pour slightly beaten eggs onto large plate; place bread crumbs on second plate. Dip fish fillets in eggs to coat; drain slightly. Dip into bread crumbs, pressing crumbs firmly over surfaces of fish to coat. Chill for 15 minutes to set coating.

2. Melt 2 tablespoons of the butter or margarine in electric skillet at medium heat; add fish fillets and sauté until golden brown, 3 minutes per side, turning carefully with broad spatula. Remove from skillet and drain on paper towels. Place fish on serving platter; keep warm.

3. Melt remaining butter or margarine in skillet; add almonds and sauté until brown, stirring constantly. Pour almonds and butter or margarine over fish. Serve with lemon wedges.

Serves 4.

creamed crabmeat

two 6-ounce packages frozen
  snow crabmeat
½ cup grated onion, drained
one 10¾-ounce can cream of
  celery soup
½ cup milk
½ cup grated sharp Cheddar
  cheese

1. Quickly thaw crabmeat in plastic bag by placing in hot water; drain crabmeat. In electric skillet, combine crabmeat, onion, celery soup and milk.

2. Cook, covered, at low heat until very hot, about 10 minutes. Sprinkle with grated cheese. Cover and cook 2 minutes longer, just until cheese is melted.

Serves 4.

Note: Or place crab mixture in lightly greased 1-quart casserole; sprinkle with grated cheese. Bake at 350° F for 20 minutes or until hot. This saves energy if the oven is used to cook something else at the same time.

skillet scampi

2 tablespoons vegetable oil
2 tablespoons butter or
  margarine
2 cloves garlic, finely chopped
2 pounds large shrimp, shelled
  and deveined
1 teaspoon salt
½ teaspoon pepper
½ cup chopped parsley
¼ cup lemon juice

1. Heat oil and butter or margarine in electric skillet at medium-high heat until ripples form on surface of fat. Add garlic; cook for 30 seconds, stirring constantly.

2. Add shrimp and cook until shrimp turn pink and curl, about 7 minutes, stirring constantly. Add salt and pepper; cook 2 minutes longer.

3. Stir in chopped parsley and lemon juice; heat, stirring constantly, 2 minutes longer.

Serves 4.

savory chinese omelet

6 eggs, well beaten

1 cup bean sprouts, rinsed and drained

½ cup finely chopped cooked pork

½ cup finely chopped onion

¼ cup finely chopped celery

1 tablespoon soy sauce

2 tablespoons vegetable oil

1. In medium bowl, combine beaten eggs, bean sprouts, pork, onion, celery and soy sauce with fork.

2. Heat oil in electric skillet at low heat; pour in egg mixture. Stir constantly until mixture thickens and is shiny and moist.

3. Cook for 1 minute without stirring to brown underside. Using broad spatula, fold omelet into thirds. Serve with cooked rice.

Serves 4.

scrambled eggs and mushrooms

2 tablespoons butter or margarine

1 cup thinly sliced mushrooms

¼ cup dry white wine

8 eggs

¾ teaspoon salt

¼ teaspoon pepper

buttered toast points

2 tablespoons chopped parsley

1. Melt butter or margarine in electric skillet at medium heat; add mushrooms and sauté for about 2 minutes, stirring constantly. Add wine; simmer for 1 minute.

2. Lightly beat eggs with salt and pepper; add to skillet. Reduce heat to low; stir egg mixture gently with fork until thickened, shiny and moist, about 3 minutes. Serve over hot buttered toast points; sprinkle with parsley.

Serves 4.

noodles florentine

one 8-ounce package egg noodles

1 envelope chicken powder concentrate

⅓ cup water

one 10-ounce package frozen chopped broccoli

1 cup ricotta or small curd cottage cheese

¼ cup grated Parmesan cheese

freshly ground black pepper

1. Cook noodles according to label directions; drain and set aside.

2. Meanwhile, heat chicken concentrate and water in electric skillet at low heat until powder is dissolved. Add broccoli; cook, covered, until broccoli is tender. Pour any cooking liquid from skillet.

3. Gently add cooked noodles, ricotta or cottage cheese and Parmesan cheese to broccoli. Heat, covered, until very hot. Serve with freshly ground black pepper over all.

Serves 4.

fried cheese with spinach balls

2 cups cooked chopped spinach, drained (two 10-ounce packages frozen spinach)

1 cup fresh bread crumbs

¼ cup grated Parmesan cheese

2 tablespoons grated onion

1 clove garlic, crushed

1 egg, beaten

2 tablespoons butter or margarine, melted

2 cups dry seasoned bread crumbs

2 eggs

¼ cup milk

four ¼-inch-thick slices mozzarella cheese

vegetable oil

1. In medium bowl, combine drained spinach with fresh bread crumbs, Parmesan cheese, onion, garlic, beaten egg and melted butter or margarine. Let stand for 15 minutes.

2. Shape mixture into walnut-size balls; roll in some of the dry bread crumbs to coat. Chill quickly.

3. Beat eggs with milk; dip each spinach ball in mixture, then coat again with dry bread crumbs. Press bread crumbs firmly onto spinach balls. Chill.

4. Dip mozzarella cheese slices in dry bread crumbs, egg-milk mixture and again in bread crumbs to make a firm coating. Chill.

5. Pour oil into electric skillet to depth of ¾ inch. Heat at medium heat until faint ripples form on surface of oil. Add spinach balls and fry until golden brown, about 3 to 4 minutes. Remove from skillet with slotted spoon; keep warm.

6. Quickly add mozzarella cheese slices to same skillet; fry until slices are golden brown, about 2 minutes. Serve mozzarella slices and spinach balls immediately.

Serves 4.

company artichokes

one 14-ounce can artichoke hearts, drained

½ cup dry seasoned bread crumbs

¼ cup grated Parmesan cheese

2 eggs, slightly beaten

½ teaspoon salt

¼ teaspoon pepper

2 tablespoons vegetable oil

½ cup prepared spaghetti sauce

four ¼-inch-thick slices mozzarella cheese

1. Finely chop drained artichoke hearts; combine with bread crumbs, Parmesan cheese, slightly beaten eggs, salt and pepper in medium bowl. Shape into four patties, each 3 inches in diameter.

2. Heat oil in electric skillet at medium-high heat; add patties and sauté on both sides until crisp and brown. Place 2 tablespoons spaghetti sauce on top of each patty; top each patty with slice of mozzarella cheese.

3. Reduce heat to low; cook, covered, for 2 to 3 minutes to heat sauce and melt cheese slightly.

Serves 4.

fried artichoke hearts

two 10-ounce packages frozen
   artichoke hearts
2 eggs
⅓ cup milk
1 cup dry seasoned bread
   crumbs
2 tablespoons grated
   Parmesan cheese
vegetable oil
lemon wedges

1. Cook artichoke hearts according to label directions; drain and set aside to cool.

2. In medium bowl, beat together eggs and milk. Place mixture of bread crumbs and grated cheese in shallow dish. Place 4 to 5 artichokes on slotted spoon and dip into egg mixture to coat; drain slightly. Roll in bread crumb mixture to coat completely. Set artichoke hearts on baking sheet; chill for at least 30 minutes to firm coating.

3. Pour oil into electric skillet to depth of ½ inch. Heat at medium heat until surface of oil ripples and has very faint haze.

4. Add half of artichokes and fry for 3 to 4 minutes. Remove from oil with slotted spoon; drain on paper towels. Repeat with remaining artichokes. Serve immediately; garnish with lemon wedges.

Serves 4.

russian beets

2 tablespoons butter or
   margarine
2 cups thinly sliced mushrooms
1 cup finely chopped onion
two 16-ounce cans sliced beets,
   drained
1 cup sour cream
¼ cup lemon juice
1 tablespoon grated lemon
   rind

1. Melt butter or margarine in large skillet over low heat; add mushrooms and onion and sauté for 2 minutes. Cover and simmer for 2 to 3 minutes.

2. Stir in drained beets, sour cream, lemon juice and lemon rind. Heat, covered, for 2 to 3 minutes or until very hot; do not boil.

3. Serve half of beet mixture hot, as a vegetable to accompany pork, ham or main-dish salad.

To serve cold: Cool and chill remaining beet mixture. Serve as salad on bed of lettuce leaves; sprinkle with 2 tablespoons snipped fresh dill.

Each half serves 4.

skillet-fried eggplant

1 medium eggplant
2 eggs
⅓ cup milk
1 cup dry seasoned bread crumbs
¼ cup vegetable oil
2 tablespoons butter or margarine
1 teaspoon salt
½ teaspoon pepper
lemon wedges

1. Wash eggplant; dry and cut crosswise into ¼-inch-thick slices.

2. Beat together eggs and milk; pour onto plate. Place bread crumbs on another plate. Dip eggplant slices into egg mixture to coat; drain slightly. Dip into bread crumbs to coat both sides, pressing crumbs to coat evenly. Place coated slices on baking sheet; chill for about 15 minutes to set coating.

3. Heat 2 tablespoons of the oil and 1 tablespoon of the butter or margarine in electric skillet at medium heat. Add a few eggplant slices and sauté until brown, about 2 minutes per side. Remove slices as browned and drain on paper towels; sprinkle with salt and pepper and keep warm. Sauté remaining eggplant in remaining oil and butter or margarine. Serve with lemon wedges.

Serves 4.

skillet potatoes

one 29-ounce can small whole potatoes
1 teaspoon salt
½ teaspoon pepper
¼ cup vegetable oil
1 clove garlic, slivered
¼ cup chopped parsley

1. Rinse potatoes well under cold running water; pat dry on paper towels. Sprinkle on all sides with salt and pepper.

2. Heat oil in electric skillet at medium heat; add garlic and brown. Add potatoes and sauté for about 5 to 7 minutes, turning to brown all sides. Remove from skillet with slotted spoon. Sprinkle with parsley.

Serves 4.

Note: Or save energy by cooking potato mixture in 8 x 8 x 2-inch pan alongside a roast.

stir-fried chinese vegetables

2 tablespoons vegetable oil

2 cups julienne strips green pepper

2 cups julienne strips red pepper

1 cup thinly sliced celery

1 cup thinly sliced mushrooms

1 cup bean sprouts, rinsed and drained

½ cup thinly sliced green onions

2 tablespoons lemon juice

1½ teaspoons salt

½ teaspoon pepper

1. Heat oil in electric skillet at medium-high heat; add green pepper, red pepper and celery and sauté for 3 minutes, tossing constantly with two wooden spoons.

2. Add mushrooms, bean sprouts and green onions. Sauté 2 minutes longer, stirring constantly. Sprinkle with lemon juice, salt and pepper; cook 1 minute longer.

Serves 4. Shown on page 70.

Note: This dish tastes superior when all vegetables except mushrooms are prepared separately, placed in plastic bags and frozen overnight.

skillet apple slices

¼ cup butter or margarine

one 20-ounce can sliced apples, drained

½ cup golden raisins

½ cup snipped dates

2 tablespoons lemon juice

2 teaspoons grated lemon rind

1 teaspoon cinnamon

1. Melt butter or margarine in electric skillet at medium heat; add drained apple slices, raisins, dates, lemon juice, lemon rind and cinnamon. Toss very gently.

2. Reduce heat to low and simmer, covered, until apples and raisins are very hot, about 10 minutes. Serve alongside pork or ham.

Serves 4.

Note: Or save energy by combining ingredients in 8 x 8 x 2-inch pan and heating in oven alongside meat for 20 minutes.

slow cooker

Slow, really slow cooking is nothing new. In grandmother's day, most children grew up with the notion that stoves had three burners and a soup pot. Nowadays, many young adults don't consider their new kitchen complete unless it includes a slow cooker. And many working women count it among their blessings. Modern versions are made of heatproof materials and a separate electric trivet. Because the slow cooker can safely simmer ingredients at low heat for several hours, you can leave for work or an outing in the morning and return to a home-cooked, ready-to-eat meal. And one-pot cooking means speedy cleanup for you—important after a busy day. As an added advantage, your slow cooker tenderizes meat without shrinking it—perfect for thrifty cuts. It's a three-in-one saver of time, money and energy.

Classic soups and stews are not the only dishes that benefit from slow cooking; you'll enjoy Veal Hungaria, Sweet and Sour Chicken, even Slow-Cook Spinach ''Quiche'' and a host of other delightfully tempting main courses. There are lots of ways to use slow cookers, depending upon their temperature ranges. Some even double as deep fryers.

Grandmother's soup pot never really went away—it's been reincarnated as a slow cooker!

slow-simmer beef stew

2 pounds beef chuck steak
½ cup flour
½ teaspoon cayenne pepper
8 slices bacon
4 cups sliced potatoes, in
   ¼-inch slices
2 cups thinly sliced carrots
1 cup sliced mushrooms
2 medium onions, quartered

SAUCE

¼ cup cornstarch
one .75-ounce envelope onion
   soup mix
2 cups tomato juice
1 cup red Burgundy wine

BOUQUET GARNI

1 clove garlic, slivered
1 bay leaf
5 cloves

1. Wipe steak well with damp paper towels; cut meat into 1-inch cubes. Toss with mixture of flour and cayenne pepper to coat well; set aside.

2. Fry bacon in large skillet over medium heat until crisp. Drain on paper towels; crumble and set aside.

3. Place potatoes, carrots, mushrooms and onions in 5-quart slow cooker. Sprinkle with crumbled bacon; place meat cubes on top.

4. To make sauce, blend together cornstarch and onion soup mix in small bowl. Add tomato juice and wine, stirring to keep mixture smooth. Pour over meat.

5. To make bouquet garni, secure garlic, bay leaf and cloves in small piece of cheesecloth. Place deep in center of stew. Cook, covered, on low setting for 8 to 10 hours or on high setting for 5 to 6 hours.

Serves 4.

beef and bean stew

2-pound boneless beef chuck
   roast
¼ cup flour
1 teaspoon salt
½ teaspoon chili powder
¼ teaspoon paprika
3 cups thin onion rings
two 10½-ounce cans red kidney
   beans, drained
one 12-ounce can beer
one 8-ounce can tomato sauce
1 tablespoon cider vinegar
1 teaspoon sugar
1 clove garlic, crushed

1. Wipe meat well with damp paper towels. Cut meat into 1-inch cubes; place in bottom of 5-quart slow cooker. Sprinkle with flour, salt, chili powder and paprika; toss to coat meat.

2. Add onion rings and drained kidney beans to meat in slow cooker; stir gently to combine. Stir in beer, tomato sauce, vinegar, sugar and garlic. Cook, covered, on low setting for 8 to 10 hours or until beef is tender.

Serves 4.

hearty sweet beef soup

2½-pound beef brisket
¼ cup water
¼ cup oil
¼ cup soy sauce
¼ cup honey
¼ cup chopped onion
2 tablespoons vinegar
½ teaspoon ginger
1 clove garlic, crushed
4 cups cubed peeled potatoes
1½ cups diced carrots
3 small onions, peeled and quartered
one 10½-ounce can beef bouillon

1. Wipe beef brisket well with damp paper towels; trim off and discard surplus fat. Set beef aside.

2. In large bowl, combine water, oil, soy sauce, honey, onion, vinegar, ginger and garlic. Add beef; turn in marinade to coat. Cover and marinate in refrigerator overnight.

3. The next day, place potatoes, carrots and onions over bottom of 5-quart slow cooker. Remove meat from marinade; reserve marinade. Place beef on top of vegetables.

4. Mix beef bouillon with reserved marinade. Pour over meat. Cook, covered, on low setting for 8 to 10 hours or on high setting for 4 to 5 hours. Remove meat; cut into cubes. Return beef to cooker.

Serves 4.

piquant meatballs with peaches

1½ pounds ground beef
½ cup dry unseasoned bread crumbs
1 teaspoon salt
½ teaspoon pepper
¼ teaspoon thyme
1 egg, beaten
¼ cup butter or margarine
1 cup thinly sliced mushrooms
¾ cup uncooked long-grain rice
½ cup chopped onion
½ cup chopped green pepper
1½ cups water
1 cup applesauce
2 tablespoons brown sugar
2 tablespoons cider vinegar
1 tablespoon soy sauce
¼ teaspoon ginger
one 8-ounce can sliced peaches, drained and chopped

1. In large bowl, combine ground beef, bread crumbs, salt, pepper, thyme and beaten egg; mix well. Shape into 1½-inch meatballs.

2. Melt 2 tablespoons of the butter or margarine in large skillet over medium heat; add meatballs and sauté for about 5 minutes, turning to brown all sides. Remove meatballs from skillet with slotted spoon and set aside.

3. Add remaining 2 tablespoons butter or margarine to drippings in skillet. Reduce heat to low; add mushrooms, rice, onion and green pepper and sauté for 5 minutes, stirring constantly. Place vegetables over bottom of slow cooker. Blend in water, applesauce, brown sugar, vinegar, soy sauce and ginger.

4. Add meatballs to slow cooker. Cook, covered, on low setting for 7 hours, adding peaches 30 minutes before end of cooking time.

Serves 4.

meatballs in wine sauce

1½ pounds ground beef

1 cup dry seasoned bread crumbs

⅓ cup finely chopped onion

1 clove garlic, crushed

2 eggs, beaten

1 tablespoon Worcestershire sauce

2 tablespoons butter or margarine

SAUCE

2 tablespoons butter or margarine

¼ pound small whole mushrooms

one 10¾-ounce can golden mushroom soup

½ cup dry red wine

2 tablespoons ketchup

1 tablespoon Worcestershire sauce

one 10-ounce package small frozen onions

¼ cup cornstarch

½ cup water

1. In large bowl, combine ground beef, bread crumbs, onion, garlic, beaten eggs and 1 tablespoon Worcestershire sauce; mix well. Shape into 1½-inch meatballs.

2. Melt 2 tablespoons butter or margarine in large skillet over medium heat; add meatballs and sauté for about 5 minutes, turning to brown all sides. Remove from skillet with slotted spoon and set aside.

3. To make sauce, add 2 tablespoons butter or margarine to drippings in skillet; add mushrooms and sauté for about 4 minutes, stirring occasionally. Blend in mushroom soup, wine, ketchup and 1 tablespoon Worcestershire sauce. Add frozen onions; simmer, covered, for 2 minutes to thaw.

4. In small bowl, blend together cornstarch and water; stir into sauce mixture. Bring to boiling point, stirring constantly.

5. Place meatballs in bottom of 5-quart slow cooker; pour sauce over meat. Cook, covered, on low setting for 5 hours.

Serves 4.

◎ *EnergySaving Tip:* One-dish meals are great energy conservers because they use only one appliance. Meatballs—excellent entrées when accompanied by rice or noodles—can easily be transformed into complete one-dish dinners. Make Meatballs in Wine Sauce as directed and stir in one 10-ounce package frozen whole kernel corn and one 10-ounce package frozen baby lima beans along with 1 teaspoon salt 2 hours before you plan to serve dinner. Not only will your one-dish meal save on the gas or electricity that would have been used for cooking side dishes, it will save on your energy too—you'll have fewer dishes to wash after dinner!

veal hungaria

1½ pounds veal shoulder
⅓ cup flour
½ teaspoon salt
¼ teaspoon pepper
¼ teaspoon paprika
½ cup vegetable oil
2 cups sliced mushrooms
½ cup chopped onion
½ cup chopped celery
1¼ cups uncooked long-grain rice
¼ cup chopped parsley
one 10¾-ounce can cream of asparagus soup
one 10¾-ounce can chicken broth
⅔ cup water
2 cups sour cream

1. Wipe veal shoulder well with damp paper towels; cut meat into 1-inch cubes. In medium bowl, combine flour, salt, pepper and paprika. Toss meat in flour mixture to coat well.

2. Heat 2 tablespoons of the oil in large skillet over medium heat; add veal cubes and sauté, turning to brown all sides. Remove from skillet with slotted spoon and set aside.

3. Add remaining ¼ cup oil to drippings in skillet; add mushrooms, onion and celery and sauté for about 5 minutes, stirring constantly. Stir in rice and parsley; cook 2 minutes longer.

4. Place vegetable-rice mixture in 5-quart slow cooker. Add veal. Stir in asparagus soup, chicken broth and water. Mix well.

5. Cook, covered, on low setting for 6 to 8 hours. Stir in sour cream; heat for 10 minutes before serving.

Serves 4.

curried lamb pilaf

1 pound lean lamb shoulder
½ cup vegetable oil
1 cup finely chopped mushrooms
1 cup finely chopped onion
1 clove garlic, crushed
1¼ cups uncooked long-grain rice
½ cup thinly sliced carrot
1 tablespoon curry powder
1 tablespoon honey
1 teaspoon salt
¼ teaspoon sage
one 28-ounce can stewed tomatoes
1 cup dry white wine
2 tablespoons flaked coconut
2 cups sour cream

1. Wipe lamb well with damp paper towels; cut meat into 1-inch cubes. Heat ¼ cup of the oil in large skillet over medium heat; add meat and sauté for about 5 minutes, turning to brown all sides. Remove from skillet with slotted spoon and set aside.

2. Add remaining ¼ cup oil to drippings in skillet; add mushrooms, onion and garlic and sauté until mushrooms and onion are tender, about 4 minutes. Stir in rice, carrot, curry, honey, salt and sage; sauté 2 minutes longer, stirring constantly.

3. Place rice mixture over bottom of 5-quart slow cooker. Place lamb on top of rice. Add stewed tomatoes, white wine and coconut; stir to mix well.

4. Cook, covered, on low setting for 8 hours or on high setting for 4 hours. Stir in sour cream; heat for 10 minutes before serving.

Serves 4.

slow slow lamb stew

4 lamb shoulder chops, ½ inch
  thick
2 teaspoons salt
1 teaspoon sugar
½ teaspoon pepper
2 slices bacon
4 cups sliced potatoes, in
  ¼-inch slices
2 cups julienne strips carrots
1 cup sliced mushrooms
1 cup sliced peeled turnip
½ cup chopped onion
½ teaspoon dried mint leaves
1 cup dry white wine

1. Wipe lamb well with damp paper towels. Sprinkle both sides of chops with 1 teaspoon of the salt, the sugar and ¼ teaspoon of the pepper; set aside.

2. Fry bacon in small skillet over medium heat until crisp. Drain on paper towels; crumble and set aside.

3. Place potatoes, carrots, mushrooms, turnip and onion in 5-quart slow cooker. Season with remaining 1 teaspoon salt, the mint and remaining ¼ teaspoon pepper. Stir in wine and crumbled bacon.

4. Place seasoned chops on top of vegetables. Cook, covered, on low setting for 7 hours or on high setting for 3½ hours.

5. Remove lamb chops from slow cooker; cut meat into bite-size pieces, discarding fat and bone. Return meat to slow cooker and cook on low setting 1 hour longer.

Serves 4.

  EnergySaving Tip: Prepare ahead! There are innumerable ways to save energy simply by thinking ahead and preparing ingredients in advance. For example, thawing frozen meat, fish, vegetables and fruits in their packages overnight in the refrigerator will preclude turning on the microwave oven to thaw them, and will cut down on cooking time. The same holds true for frozen leftover casseroles and sauces, many of which can thaw at room temperature before you reheat them in the oven or in a saucepan. Vegetables and meats will cook more quickly and thus save on fuel bills if they are sliced thinly and/or diced finely. While you're slicing and dicing, take a few extra minutes to chop up some fresh herbs like parsley or basil to season whatever dish you're making. Remember that you'll need twice the amount of a fresh herb as you will a dried herb (for example, 1 tablespoon chopped fresh parsley is the equivalent of 1½ teaspoons dried parsley flakes). All this cutting and chopping entails some forethought and advance preparation time, but it's more than worth the effort in terms of energy savings.

pork chops and stuffing

4 pork double loin chops,
  1 inch thick

½ teaspoon pepper

2 tablespoons vegetable oil

STUFFING

⅓ cup water

⅓ cup butter or margarine

3 cups packaged corn bread
  stuffing mix

1 cup finely chopped
  mushrooms

½ cup finely chopped onion

½ cup finely chopped celery

one 8-ounce can whole kernel
  corn, drained

1. Wipe pork well with damp paper towels; trim off and discard surplus fat from edges of each chop. Lightly sprinkle all surfaces of chops with pepper.

2. Heat oil in large skillet over medium heat; add chops and brown, about 4 to 5 minutes per side. Set aside.

3. To make stuffing, heat water and ¼ cup of the butter or margarine in medium saucepan until fat is melted. Stir in stuffing mix, mushrooms, onion, celery and drained corn.

4. Melt remaining 1½ tablespoons butter or margarine in 5-quart slow cooker on high setting; use to brush sides of slow cooker. Spread stuffing over bottom of slow cooker. Arrange pork chops on top. Cook, covered, on low setting for 8 to 10 hours.

Serves 4.

corn and sausage casserole

½ pound herb-seasoned
  sausages

1 cup sliced mushrooms

½ cup chopped onion

¼ cup chopped green pepper

one 10-ounce package frozen
  whole kernel corn

¼ cup chopped parsley

2 tablespoons butter or
  margarine

4 eggs

½ cup milk

2 cups grated Swiss cheese

1 teaspoon salt

½ teaspoon pepper

one 8-ounce package
  refrigerator crescent rolls

1. Prick sausages well with fork; cut into quarters. Sauté sausages in large skillet over low heat until golden brown, about 10 minutes, turning to brown all sides. Remove from skillet with slotted spoon and set aside.

2. Add mushrooms, onion and green pepper to fat in skillet; sauté until tender, about 5 minutes, stirring constantly.

3. Add frozen corn and parsley. Cook, covered, for 2 to 3 minutes, until corn is thawed. Stir occasionally to break up corn.

4. Meanwhile, melt butter or margarine in 5-quart slow cooker on high setting; use to brush sides of slow cooker. Place vegetables over bottom.

5. In medium bowl, beat together eggs and milk; beat in grated cheese, salt and pepper. Pour mixture over vegetables in slow cooker. Stir to mix well.

6. Arrange 4 of the crescent rolls in ring around outside edge of slow cooker. (Do not place in center; they will not bake.) Cook, covered, on high setting for 3 hours.

Serves 4.

Note: Bake remaining crescent rolls according to label directions. Serve with casserole.

barbecued pork sandwiches

3-pound pork loin roast

1 teaspoon salt

¼ teaspoon pepper

1 cup thinly sliced mushrooms

½ cup thin onion rings

1 cup chicken broth

2 tablespoons butter or margarine

¼ cup chopped onion

1 clove garlic, crushed

1 cup ketchup

1 cup water

¼ cup white vinegar

2 tablespoons brown sugar

2 tablespoons Worcestershire sauce

1 teaspoon celery seed

1 teaspoon salt

3 to 4 drops hot pepper sauce

4 individual hero rolls, split in half

1. Preheat oven to broil.

2. Wipe pork roast well with damp paper towels. Sprinkle 1 teaspoon salt and the pepper over all surfaces of meat. Broil for 20 minutes to brown meat and remove surplus fat.

3. Place mushrooms and onion rings in bottom of 5-quart slow cooker; add roast and chicken broth. Cook, covered, on low setting for 8 hours.

4. Melt butter or margarine in small saucepan over medium heat; add onion and garlic and sauté until onion is tender, about 4 minutes. Stir in ketchup, water, vinegar, brown sugar, Worcestershire sauce, celery seed, 1 teaspoon salt and the hot pepper sauce. Heat to simmering point, stirring constantly; set sauce aside.

5. Remove cooked meat from slow cooker; cool slightly. Cut into bite-size pieces, discarding all fat. Pour liquid from slow cooker, reserving for soup or other use.

6. Add meat and sauce to vegetables in cooker; stir to coat meat with sauce. Cook, covered, on low setting for 1 hour. Spoon mixture over split hero rolls.

Serves 4 to 6.

easy pot au feu

2 cups chopped onions
1 cup thinly sliced celery
1 cup thinly sliced carrots
2 cloves garlic, crushed
3 envelopes beef powder
  concentrate
1 teaspoon salt
½ teaspoon pepper
3 cups water
4 small pork chops
4 chicken breast halves
¼ cup chopped parsley
¼ cup prepared horseradish

1. In 5-quart slow cooker, combine onions, celery, carrots, garlic, beef concentrate, salt and pepper. Add water and stir to blend well.

2. Wipe pork chops with damp paper towels; place on top of vegetables. Wash chicken breast halves well under cold running water; pat dry with paper towels. Add to slow cooker. Cook, covered, on high setting for 8 hours.

3. To serve, remove meat and vegetables from slow cooker with slotted spoon; place on serving platter and keep warm. Skim fat from broth remaining in slow cooker. Serve broth as soup, sprinkling with parsley. Serve meat and vegetables separately with horseradish.

Serves 4.

chicken with scalloped potatoes

4 large chicken breast halves,
  skinned
½ cup flour
½ teaspoon salt
½ teaspoon pepper
½ cup vegetable oil
6 cups sliced potatoes, in
  ¼-inch slices
1 cup chopped onion
½ cup chopped celery
½ cup chopped mushrooms
3 tablespoons butter or
  margarine
1 cup chicken broth

1. Wash chicken well under cold running water; pat dry with paper towels. In large, clean brown paper or plastic bag, mix flour, salt and pepper; shake chicken to coat. Reserve surplus flour mixture.

2. Heat oil in large skillet over medium heat; add chicken breasts and sauté for about 5 to 7 minutes, turning to brown both sides. Remove from skillet and set aside.

3. Add potatoes, onion, celery and mushrooms to drippings in skillet; sauté until golden, about 5 minutes, stirring constantly. Remove vegetables from skillet with slotted spoon; place over bottom of 5-quart slow cooker. Place chicken on top of vegetables.

4. Melt butter or margarine in same skillet over medium heat; stir in reserved flour mixture. Stir in chicken broth, blending until smooth. Bring to boiling point; pour over chicken. Cook, covered, on low setting for 8 hours or on high setting for 4 hours.

Serves 4.

chicken-broccoli bake

4 chicken breasts with wings

1 teaspoon salt

¼ teaspoon pepper

¼ teaspoon crushed rosemary

¼ teaspoon paprika

one 10-ounce package frozen chopped broccoli, thawed and drained

2 tablespoons butter or margarine

1 cup sliced mushrooms

½ cup finely chopped onion

one 10¾-ounce can cream of mushroom soup

one 8-ounce package cream cheese

¼ cup grated Parmesan cheese

¼ cup flour

2 tablespoons water

1. Wash chicken well under cold running water; pat dry with paper towels. Sprinkle chicken with salt, pepper, rosemary and paprika; set aside. Place broccoli over bottom of 5-quart slow cooker.

2. Melt butter or margarine in medium skillet over medium heat; add mushrooms and onion and sauté until tender, about 5 minutes.

3. Reduce heat to low. Stir in mushroom soup, cream cheese and Parmesan cheese; stir until cheese is melted and mixture is creamy. In small bowl, blend together flour and water; stir into mushroom-cheese sauce.

4. Spread half of sauce over broccoli in slow cooker. Arrange chicken breasts on top; spoon remaining sauce over chicken. Cook, covered, on low setting for 8 to 10 hours.

Serves 4.

sweet and sour chinese chicken

2½- to 3-pound broiler-fryer chicken, cut into serving pieces

3 cups diagonally sliced carrots, in ¼-inch slices

1 cup sliced mushrooms

1 cup chopped onion

1 cup cubed green pepper

one 20-ounce can pineapple chunks in natural juice

½ cup cornstarch

one 10¾-ounce can tomato soup

½ cup cider vinegar

½ cup brown sugar, firmly packed

2 tablespoons soy sauce

1 teaspoon salt

½ teaspoon ginger

1 clove garlic, crushed

1. Wash chicken well under cold running water; pat dry with paper towels. Set chicken aside.

2. Cover bottom of 5-quart slow cooker with carrots, mushrooms, onion and green pepper.

3. Drain pineapple and reserve juice; add pineapple chunks to slow cooker. Set chicken pieces on top.

4. Blend together cornstarch, tomato soup, vinegar, brown sugar, soy sauce, salt, ginger and garlic in medium bowl; mix until smooth. Blend in reserved pineapple juice. Pour sauce over chicken. Cook, covered, on low setting for 6 to 8 hours.

Serves 4.

Note: The quantity of cornstarch used in this recipe is not excessive; slow cooking in combination with sweet-sour ingredients lessens its thickening power.

seafood chowder

1½ pounds frozen fish fillets (whiting, cod, haddock or flounder), partially thawed

6 slices bacon

1 cup chopped onion

½ cup finely chopped celery

one 16-ounce can stewed tomatoes

2 cups diced peeled potatoes

1 cup finely diced carrot

1 tablespoon Worcestershire sauce

1½ teaspoons salt

¼ teaspoon thyme

¼ teaspoon cayenne pepper

2 tablespoons cornstarch

3 cups milk

1. Separate fish fillets; wipe each well with damp paper towels. Cut fish into 1-inch pieces; place in 5-quart slow cooker.

2. Fry bacon in medium skillet over medium heat until fat melts. Add onion and celery and sauté until tender, about 5 minutes, stirring constantly.

3. Add vegetable mixture to slow cooker; stir gently to mix with fish. Add stewed tomatoes, potatoes, carrot, Worcestershire sauce, salt, thyme and cayenne pepper. Stir gently to mix.

4. Blend cornstarch with milk; pour over vegetable-fish mixture in slow cooker. Cook, covered, on low setting for 4 hours or on high setting for 2 hours.

Serves 4. Shown on page 71.

mandarin shrimp creole

1 pound shrimp, peeled and deveined

3 tablespoons vegetable oil

1 cup chopped mushrooms

¾ cup finely chopped carrot

¼ cup chopped green pepper

1 clove garlic, crushed

one 35-ounce can whole tomatoes

one 8-ounce can tomato sauce

1 tablespoon sugar

1 tablespoon Worcestershire sauce

1 tablespoon prepared mustard

1 teaspoon salt

¼ teaspoon chili powder

4 drops hot pepper sauce

3 tablespoons cornstarch

¼ cup water

one 11-ounce can mandarin oranges, drained

1. Wash shrimp well under cold running water. Place in bottom of 5-quart slow cooker.

2. Heat oil in large skillet over medium heat; add mushrooms, carrot, green pepper and garlic and sauté for about 5 minutes, stirring constantly. Add to shrimp.

3. In medium bowl, blend together tomatoes, tomato sauce, sugar, Worcestershire sauce, mustard, salt, chili powder and hot pepper sauce. Stir into shrimp-vegetable mixture.

4. Blend together cornstarch and water; stir into shrimp mixture. Cook, covered, on low setting for 5 hours or on high setting for 3 hours. Stir in drained mandarin oranges; heat on low setting 10 minutes longer.

Serves 4.

slow-cook spinach "quiche"

¼ cup butter or margarine
1 cup sliced mushrooms
¾ cup chopped onion
6 eggs, slightly beaten
2 cups grated Gruyère cheese
one 10-ounce package frozen chopped spinach, thawed and drained
1 teaspoon salt
¼ teaspoon pepper
2 cups fresh bread crumbs
1 tablespoon mild paprika

1. Melt 2 tablespoons of the butter or margarine in medium skillet over medium heat; add mushrooms and onion and sauté until tender, about 5 minutes, stirring constantly.

2. Melt remaining 2 tablespoons butter or margarine in slow cooker on high setting; use to brush sides of cooker. Reduce setting to low.

3. In large bowl, mix together slightly beaten eggs, cheese, spinach, salt and pepper. Pour into slow cooker. Top with mixture of bread crumbs and paprika. Cook, covered, on low setting for 4 to 5 hours.

Serves 4.

potatoes au gratin

6 large potatoes, peeled and cut into ¼-inch slices
2 cups diced precooked ham
3 hard-cooked eggs, sliced
¼ cup butter or margarine
¾ cup chopped onion
¾ cup chopped celery
¼ cup flour
1 teaspoon salt
¼ teaspoon pepper
2 cups milk
2 cups grated sharp Cheddar cheese
¼ cup chopped parsley

1. Place potatoes over bottom of 5-quart slow cooker. Toss gently with diced ham and egg slices.

2. Melt butter or margarine in large skillet over medium heat; add onion and celery and sauté until tender, about 5 minutes, stirring constantly.

3. Sprinkle flour, salt and pepper on vegetables; slowly blend in milk. Bring to boiling point, stirring constantly until mixture thickens. Stir in 1 cup of the grated cheese to melt; stir in parsley.

4. Pour sauce over potato mixture; stir gently to blend. Sprinkle with remaining cheese. Cook, covered, on low setting for 8 hours.

Serves 8.

Note: This recipe is a double energy saver. Serve half for one meal. Cool and chill remaining potatoes; reheat on low setting for 30 minutes the next day.

cream of mushroom soup

½ cup butter or margarine
4 cups thinly sliced mushrooms
½ cup finely chopped onion
½ cup flour
1½ teaspoons salt
½ teaspoon pepper
¼ teaspoon nutmeg
4 cups water
2 cups light cream or
  half-and-half
2 cups sour cream
one 10¾-ounce can chicken
  broth
½ cup chopped parsley

1. Melt butter or margarine in large skillet over medium heat; add mushrooms and onion and sauté until tender, about 5 to 7 minutes.

2. Sprinkle flour, salt, pepper and nutmeg over vegetables; stir to blend well. Place in 5-quart slow cooker. Using wire whisk, beat in water, cream or half-and-half, sour cream and chicken broth.

3. Cook, covered, on low setting for 4 hours. Turn setting to high; cook 1 hour longer, stirring occasionally. Stir in parsley.

Serves 8.

Note: This recipe is a double energy saver. Serve soup for one meal. Cool and chill remaining soup, then reheat on low setting for 30 minutes the next day.

mushroom-spinach filling for crêpes and omelets

¼ cup butter or margarine
2 cups thinly sliced mushrooms
1 cup finely chopped onion
¼ cup flour
¾ teaspoon salt
¼ teaspoon pepper
1 cup milk
one 10-ounce package frozen
  chopped spinach, thawed and
  drained
1 cup sour cream

1. Melt butter or margarine in large skillet over medium heat; add mushrooms and onion and sauté until onion is translucent, about 2 to 3 minutes, stirring constantly.

2. Sprinkle flour, salt and pepper over vegetables. Slowly stir in milk. Bring to boiling point, stirring constantly.

3. Place thawed, drained spinach over bottom of 5-quart slow cooker. Pour mushroom-onion mixture over spinach; add sour cream. Stir gently to blend together all ingredients. Cook, covered, on low setting for 6 hours.

4. Use as a filling for crêpes or omelets, or as a sauce over scrambled eggs, rice or buttered noodles.

Serves 4.

microwave oven

Remember those predictions for "Life in 1990" that included unappetizing prophecies of meals in a pill? Well, the future is slightly ahead of schedule—microwave ovens are the embodiment of meals-in-a-minute. But they still use good old-fashioned food. Some things just can't be improved! While extremely convenient for heating leftovers and snacks, microwaves can tackle any cooking chore your stove currently handles.

Though you needn't have an engineering degree to understand the microwave oven, you should definitely take the time to familiarize yourself with the specific features of your particular model as well as a few basic rules of microwave cooking.

Always use nonmetal ovenware; metal utensils cause arcing (a discharge of electricity) and can damage the unit. Rotate the dish according to recipe directions to ensure evenness of cooking. No one likes a two-faced cake, especially when one side is fluffy and the other soggy. Since there is no standard measurement system for microwave ovens, these recipes give cooking times in terms of percentages of power. Your owner's manual will help you translate heating requirements to your unit's specifications.

The exciting part of microwave-oven cooking is that it brings the future into the present. Because of its incredible speed and energy efficiency, you can present a Roast Leg of Lamb Provençal for eight in less than an hour. Through the microwave, traditional dishes like Sweet and Sour Pork, Barbecued Spareribs, Honeyed Chicken and Upside-Down Peach Kuchen have relocated in the 1980s without losing any of their old-time flavor or appeal. And there are other favorites just waiting to be rediscovered—check the pages that follow.

spicy rump roast

3½- to 4-pound rump roast
one .75-ounce package onion
 soup mix
¼ cup water
¼ cup dry red wine
2 tablespoons ketchup

1. Wipe meat well with damp paper towels. Sprinkle meat with half of onion soup mix; rub firmly into all surfaces of beef. Reserve remaining onion soup mix.

2. Place meat fat side down in 12 x 7 x 2-inch glass baking dish containing nonmetal roasting rack. Microwave on 70% power for 20 minutes.

3. Turn beef fat side up. Microwave on 50% power 20 to 24 minutes longer, depending on degree of doneness desired; microwave meat thermometer should register between 150° and 170° F. Let meat stand at room temperature on serving dish, covered with foil, for 10 minutes before serving.

4. Meanwhile, remove rack from baking dish; stir remaining onion soup mix into pan drippings. Stir in water, wine and ketchup; mix well. Microwave on high setting for 2 minutes, stirring once. Serve sauce alongside meat.

Serves 8.

ten-minute beef and tomato stew

1 pound round or flank steak
one 8-ounce can stewed
 tomatoes
1 cup water
1 cup chopped green pepper
¼ cup chopped onion
1 clove garlic, crushed
2 tablespoons cornstarch
1 envelope beef powder
 concentrate
2 tablespoons soy sauce

1. Wipe meat well with damp paper towels. Cut steak across grain into 2 x ¼-inch strips; set aside.

2. In 12 x 7 x 2-inch glass baking dish, combine tomatoes, water, green pepper, onion and garlic. Blend cornstarch and beef concentrate with soy sauce; stir into tomato mixture. Microwave on high setting for 4 to 5 minutes; stir sauce twice during cooking process.

3. Arrange steak slices in sauce; cover dish tightly with plastic wrap. Microwave on high setting for 5 to 6 minutes. Stir 3 times during cooking process, rearranging meat from center of dish to outer edge. Serve over hot rice.

Serves 4.

golden meat loaf

1½ pounds ground round beef
¼ cup chopped onion
¼ cup dry seasoned bread crumbs
1 envelope beef powder concentrate
1 egg, beaten
one 10¾-ounce can golden mushroom soup
2 tablespoons ketchup

1. In medium bowl, combine ground beef, onion, bread crumbs and beef concentrate. Blend in beaten egg and mushroom soup; mix well.

2. Press meat mixture evenly into 8 x 4 x 3-inch glass loaf pan. Spread top with ketchup; cover pan lightly with waxed paper.

3. Microwave on high setting for 15 minutes or on 70% power for 25 minutes. Rotate pan a half turn in middle of cooking time. Let stand at room temperature, covered, for 5 minutes before serving.

Serves 4 to 6.

beef-tomato bake

half of 8-ounce package egg noodles
1 pound ground beef
¼ cup chopped onion
½ cup chopped green pepper
one 10¾-ounce can tomato soup

1. Cook noodles according to label directions. Drain and measure 1 cup; set aside.

2. Meanwhile, crumble ground beef into 2-quart glass casserole; add onion. Cover casserole tightly with plastic wrap. Microwave on high setting for 4 minutes.

3. Drain surplus fat from casserole. Stir green pepper, tomato soup and prepared noodles into beef-onion mixture in casserole.

4. Microwave uncovered on high setting for 6 minutes or on 80% power for 8 minutes. Rotate a half turn in middle of cooking time. Let casserole stand at room temperature, covered with foil, for 5 minutes before serving.

Serves 4.

hash-stuffed peppers

3 medium-size green peppers

⅓ cup water

one 16-ounce can corned beef hash

2 tablespoons horseradish, drained

1 cup grated sharp Cheddar cheese

2 tomatoes, thinly sliced

1. Cut green peppers lengthwise in half. Using a teaspoon, scoop out seeds and membranes; cut away stem at bottom of each pepper.

2. Place peppers cut side down in 12 x 7 x 2-inch glass baking dish; add water. Cover tightly with plastic wrap. Microwave on high setting for 3 minutes.

3. Mix hash with drained horseradish. Turn peppers cut side up, and stuff with hash mixture. Sprinkle with grated cheese and top each with 2 or 3 tomato slices.

4. Microwave uncovered on high setting for 6 to 8 minutes. Let peppers stand at room temperature, covered with foil, for 5 minutes before serving.

Serves 4.

roast leg of lamb provençal

4- to 5-pound leg of lamb

3 cloves garlic, finely slivered

2 tablespoons lemon pepper

1 teaspoon rosemary

1 teaspoon salt

1. Wipe lamb well with damp paper towels. Using sharp-pointed knife, pierce surface of lamb deeply several times; insert a sliver of garlic in each hole.

2. Mix together lemon pepper, rosemary and salt; rub firmly into all surfaces of lamb. Place lamb fat side down in 13 x 9 x 2-inch glass baking dish containing nonmetal roasting rack. Microwave on high setting for 20 minutes or on 70% power for 25 minutes.

3. Turn lamb fat side up. Microwave on high setting 20 minutes longer or on 70% power for 25 minutes longer; microwave meat thermometer should register 165° F. Let stand at room temperature, covered with foil, for 15 minutes before serving.

Serves 8.

savory pork roast

5- to 6-pound pork loin roast
2 tablespoons vegetable oil
1 clove garlic, crushed
1 teaspoon grated lemon rind
½ teaspoon salt
½ teaspoon powdered sage
½ teaspoon thyme
¼ teaspoon pepper

1. Wipe pork well with damp paper towels. In small bowl, blend together oil, garlic, lemon rind, salt, sage, thyme and pepper. Rub mixture into all surfaces of pork roast.

2. Place pork fat side down in 13 x 9 x 2-inch glass baking dish containing nonmetal roasting rack. Microwave on high setting for 25 minutes.

3. Turn pork fat side up. Microwave on 70% power 24 minutes longer; microwave meat themometer should register 160° F. Let pork roast stand at room temperature, covered with foil, for 15 minutes before serving.

Serves 8.

Note: If using a microwave with only a high setting, cook pork for 22 minutes, then turn fat side up and cook 22 minutes longer.

sweet and sour pork

1 tablespoon cornstarch
1 clove garlic, crushed
2 tablespoons brown sugar
2 tablespoons soy sauce
2 tablespoons red wine vinegar
2 cups diced cooked pork
1 cup diced green pepper
one 13¼-ounce can pineapple chunks
3 green onions, cut into 1-inch pieces

1. In 2-quart glass casserole, combine cornstarch, garlic, brown sugar, soy sauce and vinegar.

2. Stir in pork, green pepper, undrained pineapple chunks and green onions. Cover casserole tightly with plastic wrap. Microwave on high setting for 5 minutes, stirring once in middle of cooking time.

Serves 4.

Note: This is an ideal recipe for using up leftover pork.

barbecued spareribs

3 pounds spareribs, cut into
serving pieces

1 cup ketchup

½ cup water

¼ cup red wine vinegar

1 clove garlic, crushed

2 tablespoons brown sugar

2 tablespoons prepared spicy
mustard

2 tablespoons lemon juice

2 tablespoons soy sauce

2 teaspoons chili powder

1. Trim away and discard fat from spareribs. Wipe ribs well with damp paper towels. Place ribs in 13 x 9 x 2-inch glass baking dish; cover tightly with plastic wrap and set aside.

2. In 4-cup glass measure, combine ketchup, water, vinegar, garlic, brown sugar, mustard, lemon juice, soy sauce and chili powder; mix well. Microwave on high setting for 4 minutes to thicken. Stir once in middle of cooking time. Set sauce aside.

3. Microwave spareribs on high setting for 12 to 14 minutes. Pour fat from baking dish; brush ribs with all of sauce. Re-cover and microwave on high setting 10 to 12 minutes longer or until tender. Let stand at room temperature, covered, for 5 minutes before serving.

Serves 4.

bratwurst in wine

2 tablespoons butter or
margarine

½ cup chopped onion

1½ pounds bratwurst

1 envelope beef powder
concentrate

¼ teaspoon dry mustard

½ cup dry white wine

¼ cup water

1. In 8-inch glass pie plate or round glass baking dish, combine butter or margarine and onion. Microwave on high setting for 2 minutes.

2. Prick bratwurst with fork. Place in pie plate with butter and onion. In glass measure, blend beef concentrate, dry mustard, wine and water. Pour over bratwurst. Cover pie plate tightly with plastic wrap.

3. Microwave on high setting for 5 minutes or on 70% power for 7 to 8 minutes. Rotate pie plate a half turn in middle of cooking time. Let stand at room temperature, covered, for 5 minutes before serving.

Serves 4.

honeyed chicken

2½- to 3-pound broiler-fryer chicken

1 teaspoon salt

¼ teaspoon pepper

1 small bunch parsley, broken into small sprigs

2 tablespoons honey

1 tablespoon orange juice

1 clove garlic, crushed

1 teaspoon liquid gravy seasoning

¼ teaspoon dry mustard

1. Wash chicken well under cold running water; pat dry with paper towels. Season body cavity with salt and pepper; fill with parsley.

2. Using wooden skewers, secure neck skin to back of chicken; secure wings under body with string. Close vent and tie legs together across vent. Place chicken breast side down in 13 x 9 x 2-inch glass baking dish containing nonmetal roasting rack.

3. In small bowl, combine honey, orange juice, garlic, gravy seasoning and dry mustard. Brush half of mixture over back and sides of chicken. Microwave on high setting for 12 minutes.

4. Turn chicken breast side up; brush with remaining honey mixture. Microwave on high setting 10 to 12 minutes longer or until juices run clear when chicken is pierced with skewer. Let stand at room temperature, covered with foil, for 5 minutes before serving.

Serves 4.

chicken in triple cream-wine sauce

2½- to 3-pound broiler-fryer chicken, cut into serving pieces

one 10¾-ounce can cream of chicken soup

one 10¾-ounce can cream of mushroom soup

one 10¾-ounce can cream of celery soup

1 cup dry sherry

1 clove garlic, crushed

1 teaspoon paprika

1. Wash chicken well under cold running water; pat dry with paper towels. Place chicken in 12 x 7 x 2-inch glass baking dish, placing thickest parts toward outside edges of dish.

2. In medium bowl, beat together chicken soup, mushroom soup, celery soup, sherry and garlic. Pour over chicken; cover dish tightly with plastic wrap.

3. Microwave on high setting for 10 minutes; turn chicken pieces over and sprinkle with paprika. Re-cover dish with plastic wrap; microwave on 70% power 20 to 24 minutes longer or until chicken is fork-tender. Rotate dish a half turn in middle of cooking time. Let stand at room temperature, covered, for 5 minutes before serving.

Serves 4.

Note: If using a microwave oven with only a high setting, cook chicken 16 to 18 minutes after sprinkling with paprika, rotating a half turn in middle of cooking time.

roast turkey breast

5- to 7-pound frozen turkey
breast, thawed

one 8-ounce package
seasoned stuffing mix

GLAZE

½ cup apricot or peach
preserves

1 teaspoon liquid gravy
seasoning

1 teaspoon water

1. Wipe turkey breast well with damp paper towels. Place turkey skin side down in 13 x 9 x 2-inch glass baking dish with nonmetal roasting rack. Microwave on 70% power for 20 minutes.

2. Meanwhile, prepare stuffing mix according to label directions. Fill breast cavity with stuffing. Turn turkey skin side up.

3. To make glaze, combine apricot or peach preserves, gravy seasoning and water in small bowl. Spread over turkey breast.

4. Microwave turkey for 20 to 22 minutes or until juices run clear when turkey is pierced with skewer; microwave meat thermometer should register 170° F. Let stand at room temperature, covered with foil, for 10 minutes before serving.

Serves 8.

Note: If using a microwave oven that has only a high setting, cook turkey for 12½ minutes; add stuffing, turn skin side up and cook 12½ minutes longer.

turkey noodle casserole

one 8-ounce package egg
noodles

2 cups diced cooked turkey

one 10¾-ounce can cream of
mushroom soup

1½ cups milk

½ cup cashews

¼ cup finely chopped onion

¼ cup dry seasoned bread
crumbs

½ teaspoon poultry seasoning

1 teaspoon paprika

1. Cook noodles according to label directions; drain and measure 2 cups. Place in large bowl; gently stir in diced turkey, mushroom soup, milk, cashews, onion, bread crumbs and poultry seasoning.

2. Spoon into 2-quart glass casserole; sprinkle with paprika. Microwave on high setting for 6 to 7 minutes or on 80% power for 8 to 10 minutes. Rotate casserole a half turn in middle of cooking time. Let stand for 5 minutes at room temperature before serving.

Serves 4.

tuna-onion casserole

one 8-ounce package egg
  noodles

one 7-ounce can tuna, drained

one 10¾-ounce can golden
  mushroom soup

½ cup milk

one 1½-ounce can potato sticks

one 3-ounce can French fried
  onion rings

2 tablespoons snipped fresh
  chives or chopped parsley

1. Cook noodles according to label directions; drain. Meanwhile, combine drained tuna, mushroom soup, milk and potato sticks in large bowl. Gently fold in cooked noodles.

2. Pour mixture into 2-quart glass casserole. Arrange onion rings on top, pressing lightly into mixture. Sprinkle with chives or parsley; cover casserole with waxed paper.

3. Microwave on high setting for 5 to 6 minutes or on 80% power for 6 to 8 minutes. Rotate a half turn in middle of cooking time. Let stand at room temperature, covered, for 3 to 4 minutes before serving.

Serves 4.

spaghetti with cheese-herb sauce

one 16-ounce package
  spaghetti

2 cloves garlic, crushed

3 tablespoons olive oil

¼ cup chopped parsley

¼ cup water

½ teaspoon oregano

¼ teaspoon basil

¼ teaspoon pepper

1 egg, beaten

1 cup grated Parmesan cheese

1. Cook spaghetti according to label directions; drain and place in large heated serving bowl.

2. Meanwhile, combine garlic and oil in 4-cup glass measure; microwave on high setting for 2 minutes. Add parsley, water, oregano, basil and pepper; microwave on high setting 2 minutes longer.

3. Toss beaten egg with hot spaghetti; pour hot sauce over spaghetti and toss. Sprinkle grated cheese over spaghetti; toss to combine. Serve immediately.

Serves 4.

lemon almond cake

one 17- to 18½-ounce package
  yellow cake mix

one 3¼-ounce package lemon
  pudding and pie filling

2 cups milk

½ cup slivered toasted almonds

1 lemon, thinly sliced

¼ cup sugar

1. Line bottom of 8-inch round glass cake pan with waxed paper. Set pan aside.

2. Prepare yellow cake mix batter according to label directions. Pour half of batter into prepared cake pan, taking care not to fill more than half full; spread batter evenly to edges. Chill remaining batter.

3. Microwave on 50% power for 7 minutes; increase power to high setting and microwave 4 minutes longer. Rotate cake a half turn in middle of cooking time. Cool cake in pan on wire rack for 5 minutes. Remove from cake pan; cool completely on wire rack.

4. Meanwhile, blend lemon pudding and pie filling with milk in 4-cup glass measure; mix very well. Microwave on high setting for 6 to 7 minutes, until thickened; stir twice during last 2 minutes of cooking time. Cool.

5. Split cooled cake horizontally in half. Place bottom half on serving platter; spread with half of filling. Top with second half of cake; spread top with remaining filling. Garnish with almonds and thin lemon slices dipped in sugar.

Serves 8.

Note: Microwave remaining cake batter according to above instructions. Cool cake completely; wrap and freeze for later use.

grape parfait pie

PIE SHELL

¼ cup butter or margarine

1½ cups graham cracker crumbs

2 tablespoons sugar

½ teaspoon cinnamon

FILLING

⅓ cup sugar

1 envelope unflavored gelatin

⅓ cup water

1¼ cups grape or cranberry juice

2 tablespoons lemon juice

1 pint vanilla ice cream

1 cup heavy cream, stiffly beaten

1. To prepare pie shell, place butter or margarine in 9-inch glass pie plate; microwave on high setting for 1½ minutes or until butter or margarine is melted.

2. Stir in graham cracker crumbs, 2 tablespoons sugar and cinnamon. Press mixture over bottom and sides of pie plate. Microwave on high setting for 1½ to 2 minutes, until crust is firm to the touch. Cool.

3. To make filling, combine sugar, gelatin and water in small bowl. In 4-cup glass measure, combine grape or cranberry juice and lemon juice; microwave on high setting for 2½ minutes or until juice boils.

4. Stir gelatin-sugar mixture into hot juice. Add ice cream, stirring until melted. Chill mixture until it mounds when stirred with spoon, about 1 hour.

5. Spoon into pie shell; chill until completely set. Garnish by swirling whipped cream over top of pie.

Serves 8.

upside-down peach kuchen

one 21-ounce can peach pie
  filling
2 teaspoons lemon rind
1 teaspoon cinnamon
one 18½-ounce package
  yellow cake mix
½ cup heavy cream
2 tablespoons confectioners'
  sugar

1. In medium bowl, blend peach pie filling, lemon rind and cinnamon. Divide filling between two 8-inch round glass cake pans.

2. Prepare yellow cake mix batter according to label directions. Divide batter between the two cake pans, taking care not to fill pans more than half full; spread batter evenly to edges. Microwave one cake at a time; chill second.

3. Microwave on 50% power for 7 minutes; increase power to high setting and microwave 4 minutes longer. Rotate cake a half turn in middle of cooking time. Cool cake in pan on wire rack for 5 minutes. Remove cake from pan to serving platter. Microwave second cake; cool, wrap and freeze for later use.

4. Using electric mixer at high speed, beat cream and confectioners' sugar until stiff. Serve alongside cake.

Serves 4. Shown on page 72.

Note: If you have only one glass cake pan, use half of filling and half of cake batter, chilling leftover ingredients and assembling and cooking in microwave oven after first cake is cooked. Cool, wrap and freeze second cake for later use.

bananas flambé

4 medium bananas
2 tablespoons lemon juice
2 tablespoons butter or
  margarine
¼ cup brown sugar, firmly
  packed
¼ teaspoon cinnamon
¼ cup white rum or orange-
  flavored liqueur

1. Peel bananas and cut lengthwise in half; brush all surfaces with lemon juice to prevent discoloration. Set aside.

2. In 9-inch glass pie plate, combine butter or margarine, brown sugar and cinnamon. Microwave on high setting for 1 to 2 minutes or until butter and sugar melt.

3. Place bananas cut side up in brown sugar mixture. Microwave on high setting for 1 minute. Turn bananas cut side down, rearranging bananas from center of pie plate to outer edge.

4. Microwave on high setting for 1½ minutes. Pour rum or liqueur over bananas; ignite. Baste fruit with flaming liquid.

Serves 4.

Index

index